"Pastor Lee's *Great to Good* is a book that needs to b _____ able. The insights and challenges will be ones that you'll return _____ over and over. The fifty short chapters encouraged, energized, and motivated me to think deeply and biblically about the most crucial issues facing our world, the church, and my own walk with Jesus. Pastor Lee's spiritual insight and grasp of history, theology, and culture, combined with decades of pastoral ministry, provide a rich and much-needed critique of contemporary Christianity and a clarion call to Christlikeness to all who follow Jesus. God spoke to me with grace and conviction through this small but *powerful* book. I highly recommend it!"

**Chip Ingram,** founder and teaching pastor with Living on the Edge

"Everyone who has a place of influence—and that is all of us whether in business, politics, church, family, or friendships—should read Jae Hoon Lee's book, *Great to Good*. The point is not that we are to give up excellence in our callings but that we are to emulate the way of using power demonstrated by Jesus. We should lead not for personal acclaim or advancement but to bring justice and blessing to those under our care. I am particularly glad to recommend this book because its author not only teaches us these truths but personally lives a life of service that reflects the goodness of Christ Jesus."

**Greg Waybright,** pastor emeritus of Lake Avenue Church in Pasadena, California

"Martyn Lloyd-Jones often said that the Christian faith is designed partly to teach people how to think. That is what *Great to Good* does. And if you will apply what is put forward, it will truly reshape your ambitions. It is one of the most practical, relevant, and stirring books I have read. This book is also prophetic, addressing the very issues that many are afraid to mention. Yes, Pastor Lee enters where angels fear to tread! He writes simply, clearly, and above all, soundly. I recommend this book that unashamedly supports Holy Scripture. This book will change your life."

**R. T. Kendall,** minister of Westminster Chapel in London, retired

"In the context of a highly competitive and success-oriented society like South Korea, it is very refreshing to read the insights and wisdom from Jae Hoon Lee, senior pastor of one of the largest churches in Korea—and the world. Lee integrates his understanding of Christian ministry with practical suggestions for daily practice. This volume provides deep insight and wisdom for Christian leaders as well as for individual Christians who wish to reshape their theological and ministerial understanding of the church and their practical life in order to shift the direction of the church from 'good to great' to 'great to good.'"

**Sebastian Kim,** Robert Wiley Professor of Renewal in Public Life at Fuller Theological Seminary

"Everyone in the church talks about following Christ, but so many of us struggle to know exactly what that means in our day-to-day life. If only we had a pearl of wisdom for every area of life! Well, thanks to Jae Hoon Lee's new devotional book, we do. *Great to Good* will not only make you think but will also challenge you precisely in those areas where the culture is pushing you in a different direction."

**Nicholas Perrin,** former president of Trinity International University

"Having had the privilege of having Pastor Lee as a doctoral student, I can recommend this book as embodying the ideal of our program: nurturing passionate, reflective practitioners. Pastor Lee's passion for God, the church, and the world pervades each page. His concisely captured insights invite reflection. His practitioner's wisdom and experience transform inspiration into action."

**David Currie,** dean of the doctor of ministry program and professor of pastoral theology at Gordon-Conwell Theological Seminary

"This wonderful collection of thoughtful essays was a balm for my soul. Encouragement, exhortation, compassion, sacrifice, and humility resonate through the book. Building on international experience and biblical wisdom, Pastor Lee has offered a remarkable spiritual gift to the global church."

**Scott Moreau,** professor emeritus at Wheaton College

"Rev. Jae Hoon Lee is a good man. Many know him as pastor of the globally influential megachurch Onnuri. Many know him currently as well as co-chair of the Fourth Lausanne Congress on World Evangelization. I know him in both capacities and more. I've seen him endure through challenges. I've seen him bear the weight and joy of leadership. And through it all, I can say that he is a good man. A man who embodies what Billy Graham described as 'the spirit of Lausanne.' A man of humility, study, friendship, prayer, partnership, and hope. It's a true honor to be his partner in the gospel and his friend."

**Michael Y. Oh,** global executive director and CEO of the Lausanne Movement

"While many would consider the various ministries of Onnuri Church in South Korea as *extraordinary*, Senior Pastor Jae Hoon Lee is a humble yet gifted servant of God who exemplifies an *ordinary* ministry. That is, he endorses a Christian life and ministry that is based on and follows in the footsteps of Jesus. Allow the wisdom of this book, collected through many years of ministry and life experiences, to help shape you and your ambitions, as you move from great to good."

**Julius J. Kim,** visiting professor of practical theology at Westminster Seminary California and former president of The Gospel Coalition

"Jae Hoon Lee is an exceptional leader for the global church. As senior pastor of Seoul's dynamic Onnuri Church—and as chairman of the host committee for the Fourth Lausanne Congress on World Evangelization—Pastor Lee's vision for global discipleship truly reaches all nations. In this wide-ranging guide to transformational ministry, he shares pithy principles for good and faithful Christian ministry."

**Philip Ryken,** president of Wheaton College

"Pastor Lee provides us with encouragement by sharing his deep love for God, inspiration from God's Word, and a reminder of the simple but clear invitation Jesus offers us to follow him and love others. Just as Jesus has been a Good Shepherd to each of us, we are now called to bring this same love, joy, hope, justice, and restoration to a hurting world."

**Gary A. Haugen,** president and CEO of International Justice Mission

"The Bible tells us that those who put their trust in Jesus Christ become a new creation! In his new book *Great to Good*, Pastor Jae Hoon Lee examines just how great the changes can be when Christ comes to live in our hearts."

**Jim Cymbala,** senior pastor of the Brooklyn Tabernacle

"*Great to Good* is a treasure trove of wisdom, insight, and encouragement for daily living. Pastor Jae Hoon Lee's collection of fifty vignettes draws on inspiring examples, well-known authors, and Lee's own years of pastoral experience in wooing readers toward humility, integrity, and service. While reflecting Pastor Lee's setting in South Korea, *Great to Good* is applicable to anyone due to Lee's international experience, broad spectrum of reading, and warm communication style. After reading this short book I feel all the more encouraged and inspired to pursue goodness—not self-promoting greatness—for the sake of Jesus Christ and for the good of others."

**J. Nelson Jennings,** editor of *Global Missiology—English*

"This is a really good book! I would say 'great,' but as the title suggests, our calling is not for personal greatness but to imitate Jesus, the Good Shepherd who laid down his life in service and sacrifice. *Great to Good* is easy to read and would make an excellent daily devotional to read alongside the Bible. It contains a lifetime's wisdom, steeped in biblical reflection and applied to everyday life. Pastors and preachers will benefit from the rich store of stories and quotes, and all readers will be challenged to reshape their values, desires, and ambitions to be more like Jesus."

**Dave Bookless,** head of theology for A Rocha International and Lausanne global catalyst for creation care

"I heartily endorse this treasure trove of wisdom (James 3:13-18), recommending it to pastors, church leaders, missionaries, seminary instructors, and others with no formal religious leadership function who yearn for spiritual vitality. It is a cornucopia of insights, advice, counsel, and admonition deeply rooted in the Christian Scriptures and faith. It is gently but persistently countercultural, showing in numerous ways how believers can quietly but effectively resist the spirit of this age and pursue a path at odds with the empty ways handed down to us (1 Peter 1:18). It is a refreshing rebuttal to the relentless pursuit of 'greatness' so frequently associated with modern churches and Christian organizations obsessed with the spirit-of-the-age-false-gospel of *more*—more members, more money, more spectacle, more attention, more fame, more pride. It quietly but effectively demonstrates that for the follower of Jesus, not *looking* good but *being* good is our calling—not *greatness* but *goodness*! The fifty short, pithy chapters contain anecdotes and insights that will surprise, enlighten, provoke, instruct, challenge, encourage, and remain embedded in memory for further pondering and life application."

**Jonathan Bonk,** mission research professor at Boston University School of Theology and president emeritus of the Global Mission Leadership Forum

"How is the outworking of embodied Christian discipleship made visible by our priorities, our sacrificial commitments, and our everyday interactions with others? This book focuses on how ordinary and extraordinary actions can lead people to glorify God rather than draw attention to ourselves. Be encouraged and challenged by these reflections from Scripture, history and modern society, and life testimonies of individuals and congregations."

**Laura S. Meitzner Yoder,** director and John Stott Chair of Human Needs and Global Resources and professor of environmental studies at Wheaton College

"In the midst of so many books about Christian leadership that stress the 'how to,' it is so refreshing to read Pastor Jae Hoon Lee's thoughtful reflections on the 'Who?' That is, the emphasis is on the character and life of a Christlike leader, not just a list of competencies and expertise. The chapters are short and pithy but full of substance and challenge. You will spend more time thinking about each one than reading it only. They constantly draw their values and inspiration from the Scriptures and especially the teaching and example of Jesus himself. Meditating on one chapter a day alongside one's Bible would be a very healthy discipline in the school of humility and servanthood."

**Christopher J. H. Wright,** international ministries director of the Langham Partnership and author of *The Mission of God*

JAE HOON LEE

# GREAT
## TO
## GOOD

HOW FOLLOWING
JESUS RESHAPES
OUR AMBITIONS

TRANSLATED BY
IRENE D. CHA WITH
JEONG-IL MOON

An imprint of InterVarsity Press
Downers Grove, Illinois

**InterVarsity Press**
P.O. Box 1400  |  Downers Grove, IL 60515-1426
ivpress.com  |  email@ivpress.com

InterVarsity Press® is the publishing division of InterVarsity Christian Fellowship/USA®. For more information, visit intervarsity.org.

All Scripture quotations, unless otherwise indicated, are taken from The Holy Bible, New International Version®, NIV®. Copyright © 1973, 1978, 1984, 2011 by Biblica, Inc.™ Used by permission of Zondervan. All rights reserved worldwide. www.zondervan.com. The "NIV" and "New International Version" are trademarks registered in the United States Patent and Trademark Office by Biblica, Inc.™

While any stories in this book are true, some names and identifying information may have been changed to protect the privacy of individuals.

The publisher cannot verify the accuracy or functionality of website URLs used in this book beyond the date of publication.

Cover design: David Fassett
Interior design: Daniel van Loon
Cover image: Spoon Graphics

ISBN 978-1-5140-1065-5 (print)  |  ISBN 978-1-5140-1066-2 (digital)

Printed in the United States of America ♾

**Library of Congress Cataloging-in-Publication Data**
Names: Yi, Chae-hun, 1969- author. | Cha, Irene D., translator. | Mun,
  Chŏng-il, 1940- translator.
Title: Great to good : how following Jesus reshapes our ambitions / Jae
  Hoon Lee ; translated by Irene D. Cha with Jeong-il Moon.
Other titles: Widaehaji anŭn, sŏnhan Kŭrisŭdoin ŭl ch'atsŭmnida.
  English
Description: Downers Grove, IL : IVP, [2024]
Identifiers: LCCN 2024006600 (print) | LCCN 2024006601 (ebook) | ISBN
  9781514010655 (print) | ISBN 9781514010662 (digital)
Subjects: LCSH: Character–Religious aspects–Christianity. |
  God–Goodness. | Christian life. | BISAC: RELIGION / Christian Ministry
  / Discipleship | RELIGION / Christian Living / Spiritual Growth
Classification: LCC BV4599.5.C45 Y53 2024 (print) | LCC BV4599.5.C45
  (ebook) | DDC 248.4–dc23/eng/20240323
LC record available at https://lccn.loc.gov/2024006600
LC ebook record available at https://lccn.loc.gov/2024006601

31   30   29   28   27   26   25   24   |   12   11   10   9   8   7   6   5   4   3   2   1

I dedicate this book to the late Pastor Yong-jo Ha,

the founding pastor of Onnuri Church,

my spiritual father, and an outstanding pastor and missionary.

# CONTENTS

## PART THREE

### CHOOSE TRUTH, EVEN WHEN IT'S PAINFUL

## PART FOUR

### DENY YOURSELF AND TAKE UP YOUR CROSS

**PART FIVE**

LIVE OUT YOUR GOOD LIFE

# INTRODUCTION

᪥

IN 2001, JIM COLLINS PUBLISHED A BOOK on business
management titled *Good to Great*, concerning the steps com-
panies had to take to be excellent institutions. This book became
a bestseller and even influenced the American church, with many
churches endeavoring to become "great" churches.

The church, however, should do the opposite. We should be
"great to good" Christians, not "good to great." The church should
strive to be good rather than great. What do I mean by that?

Jesus referred to himself as a *good* shepherd, not a *great* one.
He attributed his accomplishments to God, not to himself. After
all, God was the One who raised him up. So, the church should
follow his example of humility, service, and meekness instead of
trying to elevate itself unnecessarily.

Similarly, as Christians, we should not just stop our spiritual
growth with our *belief* in the doctrine of Christ. Through Christ
living in us, we must continue *being* like Jesus by embodying his
character. We must be people who live out good deeds like Christ,
the good shepherd. We should be missionaries who possess a
good conscience and unimpeachable character. We should not
strive for fame or "greatness." We need to strive for good.

Jesus spoke about the goodness of Christians in the Sermon on
the Mount: "In the same way, let your light shine before others,

that they may see your good deeds and glorify your Father in heaven" (Matthew 5:16).

Jesus also called us to be the salt and light of the world, but what does that entail? Good deeds.

Now, of course, only performing good deeds does not make one a good Christian. But to understand the missionary calling of the church and that of Christians is to manifest our faith in the world through our actions.

Elizabeth Shepping was one such Christian. Born in Germany, Shepping immigrated to the United States, became a nurse, and took courses on the Bible. After converting to Protestantism, Shepping answered the call.

On February 20, 1912, she embarked on a voyage to Korea, traversing the seas aboard a passenger ship and devoting the rest of her life to the impoverished and downtrodden of Korea. Gracefully wearing Korean peasant garb and men's black rubber shoes, Shepping cared for, healed, taught, and lived among the Korean people while other missionaries lived in relative luxury. She remained resolutely single and never thought to return to the United States. Eventually, Shepping changed her name to Seo-pyeong and learned the Korean language, insisting on using Korean even when using the language was prohibited under the Japanese occupation.

A beacon of compassion, she opened her heart and home to the forsaken—adopting fourteen orphans and providing shelter to thirty-eight widows. In 1934, Seo-pyeong went to be with the Lord, and even in death, she found a way to be sacrificial, having donated her body to Severance Hospital in Seoul.

During her life and at her death, Seo-pyeong was loved. But as the years passed, her name became obscure and is fairly unknown to those outside of Korean Christian circles. Shepping exemplified the life of a good Christian. She never wanted to be great, but all her life she strived to be good.

As God's sent people, our primary calling is to be this kind of good church in and to the world. This means proclaiming the gospel to the ends of the earth and letting the world witness the goodness of the gospel through our actions.

Let us look at the Korean church as an example. The Korean church has historically had a significant impact on society through the gospel, promoting societal reform such as the elimination of slavery in 1894 and the advancement of women's rights and education.

The church also provided key support for the 1919 Independence Movement, aided refugees and orphans after the Korean War, and funded projects such as leprosy treatments, tuberculosis eradication campaigns, and abolishing licensed prostitution. These transformative "good deeds" are carried out by dedicated Christians answering the call to love their neighbors sacrificially.

Martin Luther's interpretation of the parable of the Good Samaritan is a powerful reminder of how we should approach our neighbors in need. Rather than asking what would happen to ourselves if we stopped to help, we should ask what would happen to the person in need if we did not help them. This mentality of sacrificial love is what separates an event from a movement.

The difference between an event and a movement is sacrifice. As the global church continues to pursue good deeds in the world, we should not forget the importance of sacrifice. Only when we are willing to lay down our lives for the sake of our neighbors will we see a holy movement in the world. May the church of Korea be a shining example of a good church that not only believes in the gospel but also lives it out in practice.

This book offers contemplative reflections and meditations concerning how a Christian can be "good" rather than "great," focusing on self-examination in the context of the Korean church. Based on the idea of contemporary Christians embodying God's goodness in the world, this book primarily explores how we can cultivate inner goodness and engage with the global community in the pursuit of "goodness" rather than "greatness." These reflections are intended for sharing among English-speaking Christians, with the hope that together we can participate in the transformation of the world as committed followers of Christ.

## PART ONE

# IN SEARCH

# OF A GOOD

# CHRISTIAN

# 1

# CULTIVATE A GOOD CONSCIENCE

**I**N THE CLASSIC TALE OF *PINOCCHIO*, the eponymous character—a boy made out of wood—learns a powerful lesson about the enduring nature of the conscience. Pinocchio attempts to silence the cricket since it continuously nags him with moral advice, and he eventually kills the cricket, only for the creature to return as a ghost. Endlessly reminding Pinocchio to live a righteous life, the cricket symbolizes the conscience, which never truly fades away.

Deep within every human heart lies a conscience and its antithesis, which usually manifests as selfishness or a self-serving vengeance. Of these two, the conscience is the good and noble heart that God has placed within us. It guides us in our quest to know God and to live in accordance with his purpose for our lives. Although our conscience may be tainted by sin and be imperfect, the conscience still functions within us and points us toward the right path.

The Greek word for conscience, *syneidesis*, is a compound word that literally means "to know together." This word captures the idea that conscience is an intrinsic understanding that helps us understand ourselves and our place in the world. Similarly, the English word *conscience* implies a sense of knowing ("science") together ("con") with something else.

In some Native American cultures, the conscience is conceived of as a triangle within the human mind. When a person does something wrong, the sharp corners of the triangle poke through the walls of their inner selves, causing discomfort and unease. Over time the edges of the triangle become worn down and calluses form on the walls of the inner self, making it harder to feel the pangs of the conscience. This image reminds us that we must always be attentive to the voice of our conscience, lest it becomes dulled by our own neglect or stubbornness.

Genuine faith compels us to follow a good conscience. Without faith, we cannot possess a good conscience, and without a good conscience, faith cannot be sustained. Having a good conscience does not mean living a perfect life without any sin; instead, it means believing in the forgiveness of our sins through the blood of Jesus Christ and experiencing new birth, even in the midst of our sinful corruption. The power of the cross enables the survival of a good conscience and weakens the hold of vengeance within us. The Holy Spirit empowers our conscience to function as God intended.

First Timothy 1:19 speaks of "holding on to faith and a good conscience, which some have rejected and so have suffered shipwreck with regard to the faith."

Our conscience is like our eyes—it does not produce light, but it receives light. In other words, our conscience is an instrument that hears God's voice like a window that lets in light. Just as Pinocchio should have listened to the cricket, we must listen attentively to hear the sound of our conscience. It grows louder and clearer when we abide in the Holy Spirit because the living God continues to work through our conscience. A good conscience is always revealed through his work. Abandoning our conscience means forsaking our very identity and dignity while immersing ourselves in darkness.

Vengeance, on the other hand, is an evil impulse that arises from sin. It leads to rage and becomes a tool of Satan. Vengeance can sometimes disguise itself as justice. Declarations of conscience born out of dissatisfaction can actually be declarations of self-serving vengeance. Such acts, sometimes done in the name of faith, do not reflect true faith. True faith does not seek revenge. Genuine faith does not become preoccupied with religious rituals and procedures.

In the New Testament, the word *conscience* appears thirty-two times, with twenty-one instances attributed to the apostle Paul. He exemplifies a man of conscience. Conscience serves as a multitude of fearless witnesses, like faithful friends who stand boldly in front of anyone. A good conscience, as seen in Paul's life, emboldens a person to speak the truth even in unjust circumstances, without seeking retaliation against others.

When we neglect to follow our good conscience, it becomes weak. Then this weak conscience eventually becomes a withered conscience, and a withered conscience can easily be consumed by revenge. It boldly justifies evil actions and labels them as good, without any hesitation.

Governor Felix, who encountered Paul, had an opportunity to accept the gospel; however, his conscience was haunted by his desire for revenge (see Acts 24:10-27). Similarly, despite affirming Jesus' innocence three times, Pilate abandoned his conscience and succumbed to evil to appease the people and safeguard his position.

A genuine life of faith entails resolute determination and action in accordance with a good conscience. To allow our good conscience to have the final say, we must embrace Jesus' death on the cross and experience the revitalization of our conscience. "How much more, then, will the blood of Christ, who through the eternal Spirit offered himself unblemished to God, cleanse our consciences from acts that lead to death, so that we may serve the living God!" (Hebrews 9:14). Through the work of the Holy Spirit, we can restore the boldness to follow our conscience faithfully.

Martin Luther's remarkable leadership during the Reformation, despite immense persecution and obstacles, stemmed from his unwavering commitment to act in accordance with his conscience. In 1521 he openly declared, "My conscience is captive to the Word of God. I cannot and will not recant anything, for to go against conscience is neither right nor safe. Here I stand, I cannot do otherwise. God help me. Amen."

When we emulate the faith and conscience-driven lives of individuals like the apostle Paul and Martin Luther, we, too, can experience the same boldness and transformative power they exhibited. By relinquishing our desire for vengeance and attentively heeding the resounding voice of our conscience, we become living testimonies to the presence of a living God. Regardless of the injustices we encounter, our faithful obedience allows us to rise above adversity and exemplify the transformative power of divine grace.

# 2

# IT'S MORALITY, STUPID

IN 1992, THE PHRASE "IT'S THE ECONOMY, STUPID," became popular in the United States, etching itself into the minds of the American people. In that political climate, leaders needed to prioritize economic policies or their influence would fade. The real issue at hand was the economy.

People today still resonate with that sentiment. We all must submit to the power of the economy. But one must ask if this is truly the case. In this world, is it unrealistic and ignorant to instead say, "It's morality, not the economy, stupid?" Or would saying this be obnoxious moralizing?

Human nature has a terrifying tendency to prioritize rights over responsibilities. When we relinquish a right, we often desire compensation with another, greater right. Laying down a right and taking on more responsibility goes against our very nature, and few possess the mindset to do so.

The delicate balance of responsibilities and rights lies at the core of morality. Human rights can only be protected within the fence of responsible morality.

When grown children claim the right to focus on their own "needs" and consequently neglect their elderly parents, or when large shareholders shirk their responsibilities to provide for their employees and instead claim the rights and assets they believe they deserve, or when employees demand excessive pay while disregarding their work responsibilities, or when people deviate from biological reality and claim their right to sexual freedom, or when they claim the right to abortion over the responsibility of protecting life—a serious moral rift will arise. It is only by maintaining a balance between responsibilities and rights that we can ensure the protection of fundamental ethics.

South Korea, like many other nations, is like a ship facing a strong headwind because the moral fractures of society have also led to economic fractures. The costs incurred by the conflicts of social interest are enormous and hinder progress, even if they are not apparent on the surface. To address this issue, we must strive toward "maximum morality," where each member of society prioritizes responsibility over rights. This doesn't mean remaining silent when our rights are violated but rather becoming responsible holders of our rights who prioritize the welfare of all members of society.

C. S. Lewis asserted that morality is the key to unraveling the clues of the universe. He stated:

> Morality, then, seems to be concerned with three things. Firstly, with fair play and harmony between individuals. Secondly, with what might be called tidying up or harmonizing the things inside each individual. Thirdly, with the general purpose of human life as a whole: what man was made for: what course the whole fleet ought to be on: what tune the conductor of the band wants it to play.

Lewis observed that, in modern times, people tend to focus only on the first aspect of morality and forget about the other two. He believed that we must be moral not only for our own sakes but also for the sake of others.

Without taking responsibility and being willing to make sacrifices for the greater good, economic progress alone is useless. Lewis likened this to a captain of an uncontrollable ship learning how to avoid collisions; he can steer his vessel well only when his direction is clear.

To truly solve the issue of morality, we must have the courage to take responsibility and sacrifice for the greater good. Without this, any economic improvements are as useless as trying to catch a cloud in the sky. Those who are dishonest and domineering will find new ways to continue their actions under any new system.

It's not the economy, stupid.

It's our morality.

Reviving moral responsibility is the key to economic recovery and sustained growth. God is a moral God, and the church should be a moral community that shows society the difference between right and wrong. We must prioritize moral influence and responsibility more than rights.

# 3

## PAIN IS A PART OF JOY

⁂

THE FINAL WORDS OF MOSES, one of the esteemed spiritual fathers of Israel, were words from the Lord. Found in Deuteronomy 33:29, these words were directed toward the sons and daughters of Israel. In certain translations, the statement begins with "Happy art thou, O Israel."

But what grounds did he have for this statement? Israelites had spent forty years wandering in the wilderness after enduring the hardships of slavery in Egypt, and they were still facing the daunting prospect of war when they entered the land of Canaan. From a worldly perspective, the Israelites had little reason to proclaim their happiness. Some may argue that happiness is a state free from pain; by this standard, the Israelites were far from happy.

However, the Psalms remind us, "Those who sow with tears will reap with songs of joy" (Psalm 126:5). This implies that joy can exist with tears. The goal of life is not to avoid suffering but rather to endure it well and integrate it into our overall sense of happiness.

Do not be deceived into thinking that happiness can be attained by mere pleasure-seeking. True happiness is never solely for the sake of fun, as meaningless pleasure can be more painful than anything else. Happiness must have meaning and purpose to sustain it.

Once a wealthy father wanted to teach his seven-year-old son about the plight of the poor, so he took him to visit a friend's small farm in the countryside. They stayed in a simple wooden house and ate rustic food for two nights. The father later asked his son if he had learned anything from the experience.

To his surprise, his son replied, "Yes, Dad, it was amazing! We have only one dog at our house but they had four. We have one swimming pool in our backyard, but behind their house, they had a stream. We only have light bulbs, but they get to see a beautiful starry sky every night. We watch television by ourselves at night, but they sit with each other and have fun. Dad, thank you so much for helping me realize how poor we are."

Happiness cannot be found in material possessions or one's surroundings, nor is it achieved by living without pain. True happiness depends on one's relationships and with whom one shares life.

The declaration of a happy and blessed Israel in Deuteronomy 33 is based on two admissions. The first one comes from Deuteronomy 33:26: "There is no one like the God of Jeshurun." Those who can praise God and confess that there is no one like him are truly happy. The second confession is in Deuteronomy 33:29: "Who is like you, a people saved by the LORD?" Happy are those who can express gratitude and joy, saying to themselves, "Who is like me, saved by God?"

The same is true for spouses, families, and communities. Happy is the person who can tell their loved ones, "There's no one like you." Happy is the person who can say to themselves, "Who is as blessed as me to have someone like you?" Those who can confess to each other and celebrate the joy of community are the happiest.

The misery of the world arises from the pursuit of happiness through money, success, and material possessions. However, true happiness can only be found through an understanding of providential pain and a firm relationship with God, family, and neighbors.

# TORN FROM EVIL AND SET APART FOR GOOD

࿇

IN THE THIRD CHAPTER OF ECCLESIASTES, we are told that there is "a time for everything," including a time to tear and a time to mend. This idea of tearing and mending is woven throughout the Bible in how God dealt with his people. Furthermore, in the book of Genesis, we see that God created the universe through separation. God separated light from darkness, day from night, and formed the sun, moon, and stars. He tore the heavens to render time and space.

God tears and separates with a purpose. Even with humanity, God tears and separates. Throughout the Old Testament, God tore people away from their old lives to bring them into his plan, setting them apart. Abraham was torn from his homeland, his relatives, and his father's household. Jacob also experienced tearing and separation from his family. God chose Israel to be torn away from the rest of the world, to be set apart for his purpose.

God tears so that he may sew things back together more beautifully and more in line with his will. This is true for Israel and for us all. God tore Israel apart so that it might be mended together to bless the world. "All peoples on earth will be blessed through you" (Genesis 12:3) is a testament to this sewn blessing. In our own lives we may experience tearing as we are separated from loved ones through death or other circumstances. But we can take comfort in knowing that God will ultimately stitch us back in the morning of the resurrection.

Holiness requires this process of tearing and stitching. We must be torn away from evil and distinguished as holy before God. This tearing enables us to become vessels of God's salvation and blessing to others. We must constantly be fighting against evil and the forces of Satan. We must hate evil.

God hates evil thoroughly because he loves us so deeply. He wants to transform us and stitch us into masterpieces through his love, but sin ruins the beauty of his most precious creation—humanity.

Satan, with no authority of his own, sought to corrupt humanity in two ways: by tearing down our relationship with God and by fastening his own will onto us. But Satan did not succeed.

Certainly, sin tore us away from God, but ultimately God tore us away from sin and brought us back to himself through the crucifixion of Jesus Christ. He restitched humanity back to him.

Have we allowed the cross of Christ to tear away the evil in us and sew us back together with God? I hope that God may perform his great spiritual surgery on us, tearing away everything that hinders us from following him and sewing us back into Christ's love.

# A CHRISTIAN WITHOUT FOLLOWING CHRIST?

❧

ONE OF THE MOST PERILOUS NOTIONS prevalent among Christians today is the belief that one can be a Christian without fully embracing the call to be a disciple of Jesus. While Jesus accepts us just as we are, with all our flaws and shortcomings, he does not want us to remain stagnant in our spiritual journey.

In the New Testament, the term *Christian* appears merely three times, whereas the word *disciple* is used a staggering 269 times. *Christian* is not our self-designated name; it is a name bestowed on those who live as disciples of Christ. Our primary aim should be to become disciples who reflect the image of Jesus, and this pursuit demands diligent effort on our part. Only then will the name *Christian* naturally come.

Throughout history, there have been three categories of people who have failed to live out the life of a disciple of Jesus. First, there are those who outwardly abandon everything to follow Jesus but fail to exhibit his character inwardly. When Jesus and his disciples passed through a Samaritan village on their way to Jerusalem, the people rejected them. In response James and John, filled with zealous indignation, proposed, "Lord, do you want us to call fire down from heaven to destroy them?" Jesus then rebuked them for their attitude (see Luke 9:51-56).

James and John believed that those who rejected Jesus and his disciples deserved to be punished with heavenly fire. This attitude, when given a historical perspective, can manifest as a form of imperialism. Individuals holding this viewpoint perceive the world with a hostile mindset, convinced that those who reject Jesus or harbor cynicism toward the church deserve divine retribution. They seek to combat the world's animosity toward Christianity with equal hostility, pursuing vengeance and imparting punishment.

Tragically, many religious wars throughout history have been waged because of the church's adoption of this mentality found in James and John. When fire from heaven did not fall on their enemies, people resorted to kindling their own flames to punish others—burning, shooting, and hanging them in the name of religion.

In contrast, the apostle Paul taught, "The weapons we fight with are not the weapons of the world. On the contrary, they have divine power to demolish strongholds" (2 Corinthians 10:4). Engaging in physical persecution of our neighbors under the guise of religion disqualifies us as Christians since we no longer live as Jesus' disciples. The kingdom of God extends through meekness and patience in suffering, not through violence, power, and coercion.

The second category of people are those who eagerly step forward to become disciples but quickly retreat when confronted with the challenges of following Jesus. Some individuals enthusiastically offered to follow Jesus "everywhere," but when Jesus revealed that the Son of Man had no place to lay his head (see Luke 9:58), they abandoned the path of discipleship. These individuals recklessly sought to be disciples of Jesus without considering the true implications and sacrifices involved. People like this often use words such as "anywhere," "anytime," and "anything" without contemplating the genuine cost of following Jesus.

This attitude can be labeled as idolism. Those with this attitude perceive following Jesus as akin to mindlessly idolizing an entertainer. Jesus never wanted large crowds that blindly trailed after him. Instead, he desired disciples who fully comprehended the price of following him. He admonished them not to live as mere followers, superficially confessing their beliefs and sins while remaining ignorant of the one they were following.

The same crowds who joyously shouted "Hosanna!" were quick to cry out "Crucify him!" later on. Nothing poses a greater danger to our faith than broken confessions.

So, what is the price of following Jesus?

Denying oneself.

This is the price Jesus asks of those who have been saved. Though our salvation has cost us nothing, there is this price. It is our own selves that often obstruct our path to following Christ wholeheartedly. It is myself who is the greatest obstacle to living as his disciple. This is why Jesus proclaimed, "Whoever wants to be my disciple must deny themselves and take up their cross daily and follow me" (Luke 9:23). Each day I must acknowledge my sins and pay the price of the crucifixion.

Finally, there are people who, despite being called by Jesus, fail to follow him because they have not relinquished their attachment to the world. Jesus likened them to those who put their hands on the plow but look back (see Luke 9:62). When we plow the fields, we must focus on moving forward rather than looking back. A noncommittal attitude prevents us from genuinely following Jesus. This can be called nominalism, or nominal Christianity, in which one is a Christian in name only. Occasionally, when our loved ones or family members do not approve or agree, we hesitate to follow Christ, even pushing him away.

A. W. Tozer (1897–1963) identified a distinct heresy that infiltrated evangelical Christian churches. In his book *I Call It Heresy*, Tozer explained this as "the widely accepted concept that we humans can choose to accept Christ only because we need Him as Savior and we have the right to postpone our obedience to Him as Lord as long as we want to!"

Nominal Christians frequently use the word *but*: "I will follow Jesus, but . . ." As the frequency of "but" increases, the power of the church diminishes. Charles H. Spurgeon (1834–1892) termed this phenomenon a "broken confession." Despite committing to follow Jesus, many individuals break their vow by presenting various excuses and reasons. Jesus keenly observes their true motivations for not wanting to follow him, rather than the excuses they offer. Could it be that they are simply masking their unwillingness with excuses?

The urgency of the kingdom of God demands an urgent response from his disciples. It is an urgency that cannot be retreated from, abandoned, or excused. We must be willing to walk in the way of Jesus' disciples, forsaking the attitude of seeking to conquer the world with false religious pride, rejecting the blind approach of avoiding any personal sacrifice, and renouncing the disposition of a nominal believer. Nominal believers prioritize worldly pursuits and are unwilling to let go of the things of this world.

# 6

# WE REPRESENT A GOD OF LOVE

❧

THE ETHICAL LAW OF THE OLD TESTAMENT, given by God to the Israelites, commanded them to actively demonstrate love for their neighbors. God commanded them not only to love but also provided specific written instructions to actively practice love toward their neighbors. These laws of the Old Testament are of utmost importance, surpassing the laws of other contemporary societies, and they exhibit a significantly higher ethical standard compared to the laws of modern society. Particularly, love and reverence for life permeate every verse of the Old Testament.

Let us examine the words in Deuteronomy 22. God speaks of the commandments regarding respect and love for life through specific examples. At first glance, these commandments may seem casually listed without a specific order. On closer examination, however, we find that is not the case. Through detailed contemplation, a consistent flow and theme become apparent. For instance, verses 1-4 provide an interpretation of the commandment not to murder from the Ten Commandments. Although this commandment may appear to be a simple prohibition against taking someone's life, Jesus interpreted it as the love of life.

Jesus stated that being angry with one's brother could rise to the level of committing murder. This commandment reveals to us the value and dignity of life and how we should respond to our neighbors' difficulties and pains, as well as how to obey the Lord's command to love life. The secret lies in promptly offering assistance when we encounter someone in need. Have you ever missed an opportunity to do good because of hesitation? There are always good deeds that can be performed, but certain actions can be taken only if we seize the opportunities. The same applies to love. When someone is in need of love, we should extend our hand without hesitation. The timing of love is crucial, for hesitating might cause us to miss the opportunity forever.

There is a poignant photograph taken during the aftermath of the terrorist attack on the World Trade Center on September 11, 2001. The photo, known as "American Pietà," depicts four firefighters and one police officer carrying the body of Father Mychal Judge, the chaplain of the New York City Fire Department. Father Mychal, a Franciscan friar, was tragically killed by falling debris while praying for a dying fellow firefighter. The photograph is known as "American Pietà" because the lifeless body of Father Mychal resembles Michelangelo's sculpture *Pietà* in St. Peter's Basilica in the Vatican. In Michelangelo's work, Jesus' deceased body gently rests on Mary's lap.

The Italian term *pietà* translates to "compassion." It conveys looking at someone with compassion and empathy. Father Mychal embodied the concept of pietà. He sacrificed his life because he continued to pray for a dying man instead of seeking cover from the falling debris and saving himself. Could we consider his choice foolish?

If you see your fellow Israelite's ox or sheep straying, do not ignore it but be sure to take it back to its owner. If they do not live near you or if you do not know who owns it, take it home with you and keep it until they come looking for it.

Then give it back. Do the same if you find their donkey or cloak or anything else they have lost. Do not ignore it.

If you see your fellow Israelite's donkey or ox fallen on the road, do not ignore it. Help the owner get it to its feet. (Deuteronomy 22:1-4)

The message is quite clear: do not ignore it. Do not act like you did not see it. So when we encounter someone in need, we should not simply pass by as if we were oblivious. God takes notice of when we choose to ignore such moments.

A similar sentiment is expressed in the book of Exodus, albeit in the context of dealing with enemies rather than brothers. In Exodus 23:4-5 we read, "If you come across your enemy's ox or donkey wandering off, be sure to return it. If you see the donkey of someone who hates you fallen down under its load, do not leave it there; be sure you help them with it."

So, when faced with a person in need who happens to be our enemy, are we inclined to pretend we didn't see them and simply pass by? If it were a stray cow or donkey belonging to our enemy, we might be tempted to ignore it. Some might even entertain the idea of taking advantage of the situation and sending the animal to the slaughterhouse. Yet the Bible instructs us to have a loving attitude that values and cares for even the possessions of our enemies.

There are many situations where it may not legally matter if we choose to pass by without helping. Living as law-abiding citizens does not necessarily require us to love our neighbors. However, such an approach contradicts God's law. Even in those moments when we could easily overlook the opportunity to extend help, God has presented us with the law of love. The Old Testament law embodies exceptional ethical standards.

To be ready to offer immediate help in any situation, we must prepare ourselves in advance. We should not need to look for legal provisions or justifications to take action. We should cultivate a reflexive and spontaneous attitude of mind. Love manifests itself through momentary choices. Of course, there will be times when it will take a long time to express our love. However, in our everyday encounters, love must arise from the choices we make in the present moment.

When we apply the commandment to love our neighbors, we often focus on refraining from harmful or evil actions that could adversely affect them. However, this is passivity. "Not doing harm" and "love for neighbors" cannot be considered synonymous.

Jesus discusses this nuance through the parable of the Good Samaritan. The parable was an answer to a question posed by a law teacher after hearing Jesus' instruction to love your neighbor as yourself: "Who is my neighbor?" In the parable, three individuals—a priest, a Levite, and a Samaritan (the hated enemy of the Jewish people) encountered a man who had been assaulted and was in need of help. While all three were capable of assisting the victim, the priest and the Levite chose to pass by, feigning ignorance. Perhaps they rationalized the situation, thinking that touching a dead body would defile them ceremonially. Or they might have deemed it prudent to return to Jerusalem and arrange for someone else to offer aid. In doing so, they overlooked two things: first, they did not ascertain whether the victim was actually dead or not, and second, they violated the commandment to love.

However, the Samaritan responded differently. Upon seeing a person in need, he immediately extended his hand, actively showing love and compassion.

Behind the law teacher's question, "Who is my neighbor?" lies a clever attempt to find a loophole, an excuse to evade the responsibility of helping others. The law teacher sought justification for his passivity in light of the lack of clarity regarding the definition of a neighbor. When our hearts lack obedience, we challenge and question. Jesus, however, reframed the question, asking, "Who will you be a neighbor to?" These two questions carry entirely different perspectives. The law teacher's question stems from a self-centered passivity, whereas Jesus' question came from altruism.

So, what kind of neighbor should you be? It is not that we lack love for our neighbors because we are uncertain of who our neighbors are. Rather, the reason we fail to see our neighbors and their struggles is that our hearts lack the capacity for love. According to Jesus, anyone we can help becomes our neighbor. For those who view the world without love, those in need remain invisible.

Can you tell when someone in your social circle needs your help? If so, this sense signifies that you are living in accordance with the law of love. Only when your heart overflows with love can you willingly extend a helping hand to those in need.

# 7

# JUSTICE COMES FROM LOVE

꙰

IN 1948, A FATHER IN SOUTH KOREA experienced the tragic loss of his two sons through gang violence. Despite the unimaginable grief, this father chose an extraordinary path. Instead of seeking retribution, he pleaded for the life of his sons' murderer and ultimately adopted him as his own son. Pastor Yang-won Son (1902–1950) embodied the teachings of Christ, specifically the command to love your enemy. Even today, his life testifies to the transformative power of Christ's love displayed on the cross.

In September 2017, a corporal lost his life in a shooting accident during a routine procedure at a military base in Cheolwon, South Korea. Remarkably, his father stated, "I do not wish to know who fired the stray bullet. Isn't that soldier, like my own son, also a child whose parents sent him to serve in the army?" These words from the father serve as a profound wake-up call. Despite his immense pain, he displayed empathy toward someone who might be experiencing a similar anguish.

The shooting accident at Cheol-won revealed a lapse in safety management and control at the shooting range that had led to friendly fire. Notably, the military authorities, including the division commander and deputy military personnel, made efforts to console the grieving family. They arranged for the fallen soldier to be buried at the National Cemetery because he died in the line of duty. The father expressed gratitude for the unit's sincere and compassionate endeavors. While the bereaved family could have harbored resentment toward the military personnel in charge, their hearts found restoration through the genuine empathy and effort of the unit leaders, who seemed to grasp the depth of the father's sorrow.

In 2018, South Korea witnessed another powerful demonstration of Christ's love through the actions of a Seoul Central District Court judge. When a college student had posted threats on the internet to assassinate the judge, the judge made an unexpected decision. Instead of pursuing punishment, the constitutional judge forgave the student. The judge chose not to impose a sentence; however, he admonished the student, making it clear that his decision was not due to good behavior or docility. Rather, he made it clear that while the crime was serious, it would go unpunished because of mercy. This act of love offered the student a second chance to experience transformation.

When accidents occur in Korea, it is customary for everyone to condemn and demand accountability from those responsible, seeking punishment as a means of justice. This response has become ingrained in us, as if it were an indisputable principle of life. However, we must recognize that punishment alone does not make the world better. Establishing justice is not solely reliant on strict enforcement of the law. Sometimes it is the act of caring for and loving others that cultivates a healthier society.

Justice can be established only through the desires of an upright heart, and these desires are formed by experiencing unconditional forgiveness and unimaginable grace, rather than strict correction and punishment. Legalism and oppressive authoritarianism cultivate an eye-for-an-eye mindset within people, who eventually see justice as retribution rather than as restorative.

The present age needs leaders who can show that justice is actually compassionate and loving. Leaders like the father who loved the murderer of his sons and adopted him as his own. Leaders like the father who chose not to identify the shooter responsible for his son's death. Leaders like the court judge who forgave the man who threatened his life. It is in times like these that our society desperately needs hearts that are warm and filled with love.

## 8

# STRIP AWAY YOUR FACADES

M. SCOTT PECK, a renowned psychiatrist and bestselling author, observed that much of our time is spent in what he called a *pseudo-community*. In this state, we present inauthentic expressions of our true selves while we interact with others, wearing various masks to navigate the world.

Beyond mere surface-level pretenses, people put on facades to build relationships as a means to avoid isolation and rejection. This first type of mask—the mask of recognition—hides our true identity, often becoming a barrier that prevents us from truly knowing others on a deeper level. What's more troubling is that we may not even be aware of the fact that we are wearing this mask.

People often wear this mask of being worthy of recognition because they hunger for relationships and sometimes make the relationship itself the mask. Their desire for connection is so intense that it becomes excessive, resembling the behavior of gluttons. They engage in countless interactions, going to great lengths to please others, yet they never find true satisfaction in these relationships. Their pursuit is fueled by a fear of not being recognized or acknowledged. They seek stability and security through others. If you find yourself in this category, heed the words of Dietrich Bonhoeffer: "Let him who cannot be alone beware of community."

The desire for recognition stems from arrogance. Arrogant individuals are consumed by the belief that everyone should acknowledge their importance. They view relationships through the lens of the self and can build relationships only if others affirm their importance. This is the epitome of arrogance.

These individuals become fixated on superficial and shallow matters, sacrificing intimacy with God and their loved ones in pursuit of external validation. Unsurprisingly, this trajectory leads to deep-rooted emotional and spiritual problems within their relationships and estrangement.

The second mask frequently worn is the mask of self-achievement. It differs from the mask of recognition in relationships and carries its own consequences. People who wear this mask often exhibit traits associated with paranoid personality disorder or avoidant personality disorder. They believe that intimate relationships bring only pain. Consequently, regardless of who they encounter, they maintain a safe distance and erect protective barriers. They fear deepening connections with others.

Instead, they focus solely on achieving success. They believe that they must be exceptional and excel in their work to earn love and acceptance. They sacrifice relationships for success even though the validation they crave can only come from relationships.

In Gordon MacDonald's book *Ordering Your Private World*, we encounter numerous stories of individuals consumed by the unbridled pursuit of worldly success. These "driven" individuals are so immersed in their quest that they fail to invest time in cultivating intimate relationships. Apart from their relationship with God, their busyness leaves them struggling to maintain connections with their spouses, family, and friends.

These masks hinder genuine connection and prevent us from experiencing the fullness of authentic relationships. It is essential that we recognize and shed these masks, allowing our true selves to emerge and fostering relationships based on vulnerability, honesty, and love.

These two types of people share something in common: a simultaneous longing for and fear of intimate relationships. This is why they resort to wearing masks.

In Psalm 131:2 David expresses the sense of security he experiences when he removes the masks crafted from pride. He says,

But I have calmed and quieted myself,
    I am like a weaned child with its mother;
    like a weaned child I am content.

As a newborn baby, your relationship with your mother shapes all other relationships. You find intimacy and nourishment in your mother's embrace, as love and sustenance are provided together. When a baby cries out of hunger, it is also an expression of their longing for intimacy. If the mother embraces the newborn and meets their nutritional needs, the child will grow up to be emotionally stable, free from the hunger for relationships.

David's reference to a weaned child in the psalm signifies a child who can walk and speak on its own. The child's yearning for its mother's embrace to find stability does not stem from a fear of the world but rather from a desire for intimate love that brings peace and stability.

Just as we cannot resist the desire for food, we cannot reject the desire for relationships, for relationships are as essential to our lives as physical nourishment. Just as we cannot cling to or refuse food, we cannot cling to or reject relationships. Healthy relationships require ongoing nurturing from both parties, while simultaneously granting freedom to one another. Genuine, healthy relationships are not meant to exploit the other person to satisfy our own needs but rather to uplift and honor them. Ultimately, we must remove our masks to cultivate healthy, nonobsessive, and mutually enriching relationships with others.

# 9

# TRUE BLESSINGS
# OF CHRIST-FOLLOWERS

❧

THE SERMON ON THE MOUNT is not a set of laws that we must adhere to in order to gain entry into the kingdom of God. Instead, it reveals the inner nature and mindset of those who have already entered the kingdom of God while still residing in this earthly realm.

The fundamental tenet of the Sermon on the Mount is "heaven opened on earth." The Beatitudes, eight blessings outlined in Matthew 5:3-12, represent the various forms of blessings experienced by those who have entered the kingdom of God. On closer examination, these blessings are not reserved for a select few or extraordinary saints but are available to all Christians who have entered the kingdom. Furthermore, all eight are interconnected and interrelated.

The Beatitudes reveal profound truths about the kingdom of God and the blessings experienced by its inhabitants. Let us explore each and acquire a fuller understanding of God's kingdom.

***Blessed are the poor in spirit, for theirs is the kingdom of heaven.*** Those who are rich in their own spirit may think they lack nothing, but they are actually impoverished, having forfeited the riches of heaven and endangered their souls. On the other hand, the poor in spirit are truly wealthy, for they have received the kingdom of heaven. We all come to Jesus Christ in a state of spiritual poverty, but through him we become rich in the kingdom of God.

***Blessed are those who mourn, for they will be comforted.*** The world often associates happiness with a life free from sorrow, but the truth is that everyone experiences sorrow in this fallen world. This sorrow is a direct result of recognizing our poverty in spirit and grieving over our own sins. The second blessing flows from the first. The sacrifice God desires is a broken and contrite spirit (Psalm 51:17).

***Blessed are the meek, for they will inherit the earth.*** Those who mourn over their sins, starting from their poverty in spirit, become meek. Meekness is not merely strength under control; it is the provision of God's power to obediently follow his will, no matter the challenges we face. It is a heart that is soft and submissive to God's providence, not in rebellion but in acceptance.

***Blessed are those who hunger and thirst for righteousness, for they will be filled.*** Each subsequent blessing builds on the previous one. The poor in spirit become mourners, the mourners become meek, and those who stand humbly before God with meekness develop a deep hunger and thirst for righteousness. Just as the physically dead do not feel physical hunger and thirst, the spiritually dead do not feel a spiritual hunger and thirst. But when someone is born anew by the Holy Spirit, they begin to long for righteousness. True life is characterized by a hunger and thirst for righteousness.

***Blessed are the merciful, for they will be shown mercy.*** Mercy is born out of compassion, and compassion arises from mercy. What is mercy? It is lovingly reaching out to someone in distress, not turning a blind eye to their suffering. Mercy goes beyond empathy or sympathy; it actively participates in alleviating the other person's suffering. If we are merciful, we will be able to forgive others. Understanding God's mercy and forgiveness toward us should move us to extend mercy to others.

***Blessed are the pure in heart, for they will see God.*** The sixth blessing is granted to those who possess pure hearts. Throughout our lives we see countless things, but the most important thing to see is God. Those who dwell in the kingdom of God, even while living on this earth, have come to know God through Jesus Christ. To know God is to see him. When the pure in heart see others, they also see God who governs them. Even as we examine the course of history, we witness God presiding over every aspect.

***Blessed are the peacemakers, for they will be called children of God.*** To be peacemakers, our hearts must be pure and clean. James 3:17 says that heavenly wisdom is first pure and then peace-loving. This aligns with Jesus' teaching because a person with a pure heart will naturally pursue peace.

True peace is not achieved through compromising righteousness. It is not about sweeping past wrongdoings under the rug simply because both sides have made mistakes. True peace involves acknowledging and addressing one another's sins, mistakes, and wrongs before God, seeking correction and reconciliation.

***Blessed are those who are persecuted because of righteousness for theirs is the kingdom of heaven. Blessed are you when people insult you, persecute you, and falsely say all kinds of evil against you because of me. Rejoice and be glad, because great is your reward in heaven, for in the same way they persecuted the prophets who were before you.*** Jesus speaks of the blessedness of those who are persecuted because of righteousness. When we wholeheartedly live for Jesus, the world often treats us unfavorably. When our lives reflect his nature and we follow his example, we encounter difficulties similar to what he faced. No servant is greater than his master.

Jesus, the embodiment of love and mercy, experienced persecution. Therefore, we should expect to face persecution as well.

The depth of our experience and mindset as believers under persecution for the sake of righteousness in the kingdom of God is vastly different from other experiences. In the kingdom of God, being persecuted for righteousness is the deepest and most significant experience we can have on earth.

Instead of fearing persecution, we are called to embrace it for the sake of righteousness, just as Jesus did. By doing so, we gain access to and lay hold of the kingdom of heaven. We can find encouragement in knowing that great is our reward in heaven.

# 10

# GOODNESS SHINES

JESUS DESCRIBED THE INFLUENCE of the people of God's kingdom on the world through the metaphors of salt and light. He did not say, "You can become the salt," a mere possibility, or "You must become the salt," a command. He directly declared that those with the eight characteristics expressed in the Beatitudes are the salt and light of the world (Matthew 5:13).

In antiquity, salt was exchanged as currency, used to signify an unchanging commitment to keep the terms of an exchange. In Numbers 18:19 the promise between God and man is expressed as a "covenant of salt," and in Leviticus 2:13 the people are required to sprinkle salt on the grain offering. Salt was incredibly important.

"You are the salt of the earth" (Matthew 5:13) implies that the earth is so rotten and corrupt that it desperately needs salt. The world is pessimistic. The idea that the world will become more beautiful over time without intervention is a vain fantasy. The world is undoubtedly getting darker. A tasteless world needs life-giving salt.

Martin Luther understood the powerful, provocative quality of salt, stating that when applied to a wound, salt causes discomfort as it purifies. In the context of spreading the gospel, he emphasized the need to address issues directly, akin to rubbing salt into their wounds. Luther held the view that a faithful interpretation of the Bible acts like true "salt," confronting and encouraging the world to accept faith in Jesus, leaving no other alternative but to believe.

German theologian Helmut Thielicke similarly said, "Some Christians seem to have an ambition to be the honeypots of the world. Jesus did not say, 'You are the sugar of the world.' Salt stings. Salt stimulates." "Salt of the world" does not mean bringing sweetness to the world but providing much-needed stimulation and purification.

Jesus then discusses light. It is foolish to try to hide light. A city on a hill with running electricity will inevitably reveal its lights in the night even from afar. The church is a "city on a hill." Just as seeing lights on a mountain automatically tells you that there are people living there, a gathering of believers cannot be hidden.

Concealed faith is not genuine faith. Indeed, people should not practice their faith in order to be seen, but a true believer is someone who cannot help but be seen. There can be no hidden disciples of Christ. If someone does not appear as a believer to others, something about their faith must have intrinsically changed. As long as we do not abandon our faith, it is impossible not to show it. When we first believe in Jesus, we may hide our belief from others, but as we truly experience the blessings and grace of heaven, we will proudly proclaim ourselves as believers in Jesus, and others will see that. Light cannot be hidden.

John Wesley said that it is no easier to hide a Christian than it is to hide a city: "As well may men think to hide a city, as to hide a Christian: yea, as well may they conceal a city set upon a hill, as a holy, zealous, active lover of God and man."

The light that God shines through our souls manifests in good deeds. When we live out the kingdom of heaven on earth, the Beatitudes are formed within us. A person with these virtues can't help but do good deeds. Doing good deeds ensures that people focus on God and not on us. The only goal should be to ensure that everyone who sees our good deeds glorifies God in heaven. When this becomes the desire of our lives, we live out the kingdom life here on earth, we become good Christians.

## PART TWO

# A GOOD LEADER BUILDS CHRIST'S CHURCH

# 11

# BE THE BEST MAN,
# NOT THE BRIDEGROOM

"COULD THE CHURCH BE JEALOUS OF CHRIST?"

I asked this intentionally provoking question to my church members. As anticipated, their reaction was one of disbelief, completely dismissing the inquiry as utterly preposterous. How could the church—as the embodiment of Christ—even entertain feelings of jealousy toward the very One we revere and submit to, our esteemed Savior and Lord?

However, upon delving deeper into church history, we can uncover a sobering reality: one significant factor contributing to the church's decline in power and influence was, in fact, its own jealousy of Christ. This jealousy also manifested itself in the envy of Jewish leaders of Jesus' lifetime. These leaders, out of their jealous desire to maintain religious control of their community, exerted pressure on Roman authorities and ultimately brought about Christ's crucifixion. Despite their malicious intentions, Christ unequivocally revealed himself as God through his resurrection, authoritative teachings, and wondrous miracles.

Tragically, throughout history and even in the present day, this insidious jealousy is at the heart of the issues plaguing the church.

Look at when some of John the Baptist's disciples approached him with worry, saying, "The Christ you testified about is now baptizing, and people are flocking to him instead of coming to us" (see John 3:26). In essence, they were distressed that they were losing followers to Jesus' ministry. These disciples were more invested in the number of people who sought John's baptism than in their teacher's testimony. As followers of John, who was widely renowned during that time, they took pride in believing that they were partaking in something meaningful and influential. In fact, it is possible that they were using John's ministry as a means to satiate their desire for power and influence.

John's response to his disciples bears great significance for the church: "You yourselves can testify that I said, 'I am not the Messiah but am sent ahead of him.' The bride belongs to the bridegroom. The friend who attends the bridegroom waits and listens for him, and is full of joy when he hears the bridegroom's voice. That joy is mine, and it is now complete. He must become greater; I must become less" (John 3:28-30).

With this analogy, John portrays himself as the friend of the bridegroom, akin to what we might call the best man today. The best man's role is to support the groom and focus attention on him. The best man finds joy in witnessing the groom's delight as he welcomes his bride. This is the best man's duty. However, if the best man seeks to overshadow the groom and catch the bride's attention, he becomes an adversary. John, as the friend of the bridegroom, rejoiced in Christ's prominence and experienced profound joy as people flocked to him for baptism.

John's confession that, "He must become greater; I must become less," should not be John's alone. As the church grows and thrives, we must continually embrace this confession as our own. The church must diminish in its self-centeredness and magnify the person and work of Christ. This does not entail relegating ourselves to a state of financial feebleness or operational impotence, devoid of the ability to serve our communities. On the contrary, it necessitates a posture of humility and a recognition that our purpose is to glorify Christ above all else.

So let us heed this timeless wisdom from John the Baptist and embrace a mindset that seeks to exalt Christ, magnifying his name and his redemptive work. In doing so, we will find our true purpose and witness the transformative power of the church radiating throughout the world.

The church, as a unified body, possesses immense potential in proclaiming the gospel and engaging in acts of social service. However, we must recognize the paradoxical nature of the church: the more it grows and flourishes, the more it must diminish and deny itself.

In our pursuit of greatness, the church must embrace the path of self-denial, for it is through this posture that Christ is truly revealed and exalted. It is through self-denial that the church becomes a powerful instrument in the hands of God.

Let us contemplate the sources of our pleasure and the objects of our joy. Church leaders, in particular, must find their delight solely in people turning to Christ, the bridegroom. We must abide in the confession that declares, "We are not Christ; we are his witnesses."

Throughout history, we have witnessed the church's tendency to forget John the Baptist's confession, and it has become increasingly fragile as a result. Just as a best man mistaken for the groom will face rejection, the church must remain steadfast in its role as the friend of Christ, bringing people from all walks of life into communion with him.

The church is the living embodiment of Christ, a friend to him, and a community that bridges the gap between the world and Christ. Ultimately, the church will be divided into two categories: those who rejoice in Christ and those who are envious of him. The church consumed by jealousy will fade from memory, while the church that finds its joy in Christ will be strengthened in his kingdom. The purpose of the church remains constant: "He must become greater; I must become less." Have we, as the church, truly embraced the path of self-denial to reveal Christ and find our ultimate joy in him?

May the church continually strive to become less, that Christ may be magnified and glorified in all we do. It is in our self-denial and exaltation of Christ that the true purpose and power of the church will be realized.

# 12

# SIGNS OF JUDAS'S BETRAYAL

҂

ONE OF THE MOST INFAMOUS FIGURES of Christian history is Judas Iscariot, known as the Traitor. Dante's *Inferno*, a famous epic poem describing the author's allegorical journey down into hell, places Judas Iscariot in the innermost circle of hell and he must endure the most excruciating eternal punishment due to his reprehensible betrayal of Jesus. The name Judas is even used as a synonym for a traitor. Interestingly, there have been peculiar revisionist theories that seek to excuse Judas and justify his actions.

In 2006, National Geographic released a series of documentaries and media that propagated heretical views centered on Judas Iscariot. Some argued that Judas might have been a fictional character, while others claimed that ancient documents dating back seventeen hundred years portrayed Judas as the most devoted disciple of Jesus Christ. There were even accounts suggesting that Jesus himself instructed Judas to betray him and that Judas willingly took on that responsibility despite his reluctance. These proponents of Judas's exoneration went so far as to advocate for the restoration of the discredited Gospel of Judas, written in AD 180, which the early church deemed counterfeit and heretical.

Similar forms of Judas revisionism can be found in literature and art. The renowned Korean novelist Dong-ri Kim (1913-1995) portrayed Judas in his novel *Saban's Cross* not as a traitor but as an individual grappling with the pursuit of national independence for his people. Even in the musical *Jesus Christ Superstar*, the portrayal of Judas tends to romanticize his betrayal, suggesting that he was compelled by fate to do something he did not desire.

Why do historians and artists promote these views of Judas that contradict the teachings of the Bible? Perhaps they seek to find justification for their own betrayals by rationalizing Judas's actions. If history's most notorious and repugnant act of betrayal can be rationalized as a righteous deed, then no betrayal can be seen as betrayal, and no sin can be recognized as sin.

However, Judas's betrayal is an inexcusable sin. The fact that the betrayal of the Messiah was prophesied in the Scriptures does not absolve Judas of responsibility, as he freely chose to commit that act. John Calvin, the prominent theologian, aptly noted that despite the prophecy of treachery and death, Judas could not evade culpability because of his wicked heart.

God cannot be the author of sin, nor does he incite anyone to commit evil deeds. Sin is the consequence of one's own choices. Despite human beings' propensity for sin, God in his sovereignty works out his divine providence to fulfill his plans. Judas, unfortunately, willingly opened the door for Satan to enter his life. He did not resist the possession of Satan but rather invited it in. Satan numbs the voice of conscience and justifies evil actions. He deceives individuals into believing they are accomplishing good while committing acts of wickedness. Satan removes the fear of God, clouds rational thinking, erodes shame, and boldly engages in evil deeds.

Some propose an interpretation that Judas betrayed Jesus because of a shattered ideal of the kingdom of God, that he was disillusioned with Jesus' message and ministry. These proponents argue that he made inevitable choices to uphold his convictions, portraying him as a self-sacrificing figure bound to the will of an inescapable destiny.

Yet, people like Dietrich Bonhoeffer, for instance, did not use their social circumstances to commit acts of evil. Bonhoeffer prayed for the collapse of his beloved Germany during World War II, betraying his own country for a higher moral. Judas's betrayal lacks any trace of self-sacrifice. Unlike Bonhoeffer, Judas chose self-interest over self-sacrifice. He cannot be seen as a "reluctant villain" but rather as a wicked man who pursued riches. Judas was not a victim.

Ironically, even some Christians try to justify Judas Iscariot's betrayal as understandable. They criticize Jesus' betrayer while finding solace in his actions, likely justifying their own behaviors through him. People who believe this probably view themselves as righteous and will have no mercy for obvious sinners but will conveniently turn a blind eye to Judas's betrayal.

But one must ask: Can a person become corrupt despite receiving direct discipleship training from Jesus himself?

Judas serves as a stark reminder that even those chosen by Jesus can become children of destruction. If someone who walked alongside Jesus could open the door to Satan and invite betrayal, we also should be wary of similar dangers in our own lives. We must remain vigilant, especially when it comes to greed and worldly gain, because the life of Jesus—the Son of God—was only worth thirty silver pieces to Judas.

Sadly, there are distressing signs of Judas's betrayal within the church—preoccupation with numbers, worldly success and influence, and other disordered priorities. Although there may be several other reasons for this lamentable state of affairs, the underlying factor of money is apparent. Merely fixating on upholding

rigid doctrinal standards without earnestly confronting the betrayals we ourselves commit will inevitably lead us down a path
of failure, mirroring the fate of Judas.

The church must acknowledge that we betray Christ in ways
that are akin to Judas's betrayal. The model of Judas is evident in
various Christian institutions—including denominations, semi-
naries, churches, and mission communities. For this very reason,
the church has lost its social influence. We must repent and strip
away our reliance on money in church decisions, including selecting church and denominational leaders. As the church grows,
our top priority should be missions and sharing the gospel. We
must recognize the signs of Judas within us, repent, and turn our
hearts back to Christ.

## 13

# FOOLS FOR CHRIST

ॐ

HISTORICALLY, CRISES IN THE CHURCH have arisen when Christianity becomes "Christianity," a culture based on religious church practices rather than Christ. This happened with the churches in Europe and North America and is now occurring within churches in South Korea. To escape this crisis, the church must rediscover Jesus. It's not about finding the Jesus of the past as a historical figure but rather about acknowledging him as the living God and Lord manifest among us today. We must rediscover Jesus, who is trapped in our ecclesiastical systems and rituals, and restore him to his rightful place.

The church becomes a religion without Jesus because of a misunderstanding of who Jesus is. Surprisingly, even in Jesus' time, people misunderstood him. Even the disciples who lived with him misjudged him. When they looked at Jesus according to their own beliefs, ideologies, desires, and expectations, they failed to truly see him. The Jews had political expectations of the kingdom of God, leading them to desire a specific image of the Messiah. When the person who came did not meet their expectations, they did not recognize Jesus as the Messiah.

Similarly, today we can fail to truly see Jesus if we view him according to our own ideologies, desires, and expectations. If we perceive Jesus as a harbinger of material prosperity and well-being, then the church becomes a religious group seeking success in Jesus' name. If we see Jesus as a bringer of political liberation, the church turns into the most revolutionary political group in the world. If we regard Jesus as a source of human consolation, the church becomes merely a social group connecting people in need of friends. Such things may or may not be secondary offshoots of the church, but focusing solely on these aspects prevents us from truly recognizing who Jesus is.

We can accurately see Jesus only through the incarnation and the cross. We need to see Jesus, who humbled himself so much as to become human, and who humbled himself even further to die on the cross on our behalf. People fail to truly see Jesus because they refuse to see him through the incarnation and the cross. They want to view him only through the eyes of glory and blessing. The fact that someone as popular and powerful as Jesus had to die an ignominious death on the cross seems almost foolish.

The apostle Paul described the cross as "the foolishness of God" (1 Corinthians 1:25). However, the seemingly foolish cross is, in reality, God's infinite wisdom and the power that grants us eternal life. Jesus, bearing the cross characterized as God's foolishness, became a fool for us. The term *fool* denotes that Jesus became completely rejected and abandoned. The Christians of the apostolic age were Christlike figures in the world. However, they were not the glorious Christians one might expect. When they were the earthly embodiment of Christ, they appeared very dangerous and crude.

They were the ones who sat at the seats meant for the lowest caste. They became a spectacle to the angels and humans of the earth. They were lowly and humbled. They hungered, thirsted, wore rags, were beaten, and wandered around. They became like rubbish, like the dregs of the world. Yet they responded with blessings when cursed, endured persecution, and answered scorn with kind words. They chose to be "foolish fools" for Christ and through Christ. As they lived like fools for Christ and endured the crucifixion of Jesus Christ, his presence remained among them through the Holy Spirit. Thus their lives resembled Jesus Christ living physically among us in this world.

When we humble ourselves, become weak, and fully rely on Christ, the power of Christ's new life will work within us, and the power of the resurrection will manifest through us. A new life's power, which the world cannot give, will be revealed to the earth through the church. A new life's power, which the world cannot create, will appear, and the world will both fear and praise the church. Through the church, the world will come to see Christ.

## 14

# WHY IS THE CHURCH WEAK?

❧

IN THE THOUGHT-PROVOKING BOOK *An Unstoppable Force* by Erwin McManus, who was the visionary founder of Mosaic Church, we encounter not only an apt title describing the church but also a daring invitation for the church to be "an unstoppable force." McManus challenges readers to breathe new life into the modern-day church by shedding outdated perspectives and practices that have resulted in spiritual stagnation. As I delved into its pages, I found myself contemplating the early church depicted in the book of Acts—a vibrant community that embodied the unwavering power of the gospel even in the face of intense persecution. It was an unstoppable force that nothing could hinder during that remarkable era.

When it comes to the present day, however, should we attribute the church's apparent weaknesses solely to the pervasive evil of our age? The reality is that throughout history every age has been marred by its own share of evil. The decline of the church cannot be attributed solely to the corrupt environment in which it exists. In fact, despite the challenges posed by such an environment, the church may find itself better equipped than ever to fulfill its ministry in the twenty-first century. The advancements in communication, particularly with the emergence of the internet, have provided unprecedented opportunities to share the gospel with countless individuals every single day.

Likewise, we cannot claim that the church lags behind because of the rapidly changing culture. Throughout history, the church has been a transformative force, influencing and guiding culture. The root of the problem does not lie in our environment or culture; rather, it resides within the church itself. Unfortunately, the church has lost touch with the power of God. Allow me to share a passage from McManus's book, one that I have revisited repeatedly and even committed to memory.

> There is no perfect storm out there that can sink the church of Jesus Christ. No matter how much or how rapidly culture changes, the church is designed to prevail. Yet, with each culture shift, it is painfully obvious that the church has become an institution rather than a movement. The distinction lies in the fact that institutions preserve culture, while movements create culture. Many times those who attempt to preserve a dissipating culture will also join it in its ignoble demise.

The book of Acts portrays a confrontation of spiritual power. In this encounter, powerful people of the world were overcome by powerless ones. Even those who held great authority in Jewish society were unable to suppress the testimony of the apostles, who were filled with the Holy Spirit. Despite persecution and rejection, the apostles remained steadfast in their ministry. How was this possible?

First, the truth always triumphs over falsehood. The apostles taught and performed miraculous signs in the name of Jesus, proclaiming his resurrection. The religious leaders, though unsettled, were not surprised. If Jesus truly rose from the dead, their deception and hypocrisy would be exposed. Yet no amount of worldly power or force could contain the truth. It is futile to try to suppress it.

This response from religious leaders is not new; it reflects the attitude displayed toward Jesus himself. When Jesus healed a man by the Pool of Bethesda on the Sabbath, the Jewish religious authorities persecuted him for breaking their religious laws (see John 5:16). Even witnessing extraordinary miracles, they demanded explanations within their own self-created religious systems.

This is a crucial reason why the church has lost its spiritual power, becoming more like an institution than a movement. Many in today's church are more concerned with the religious systems they have built than with the truth itself. However, the truth cannot be confined within a system rooted in falsehood and vanity. If the church does not align itself with the truth, it will lose its strength and transformative power.

Second, the apostles became people who could not be silenced in sharing the gospel under any circumstances. Peter and John boldly declared, "We cannot help speaking about what we have seen and heard" (Acts 4:20). When someone cannot stop sharing the gospel, three conditions are typically present: their witness is grounded in historical facts, it is based on personal experience, and it is empowered by the Holy Spirit—an anointing from heaven. The apostles' unwavering testimony could not be stifled, because they had been transformed by the Holy Spirit and boldly preached the gospel.

Third, the apostles stood against the power of the Jewish religious authorities, not relying on the false powers of the world but on the power of God. If they had relied on worldly power, witnessing would have quickly ceased. The church faces the great temptation in every era to submit to the world rather than bring the world into submission. One notable example is from the Middle Ages when the pope's crowning of emperors solidified the power of kings. However, the church itself was far from Christlike during that time; it was the darkest period in its history.

The church does not require worldly power. The world always opposes God's work. The church should triumph on its journey to the cross in the face of worldly challenges. Victory obtained through worldly power is temporary, but victory in Christ is eternal. Our faith should be the power that overcomes the world. With Jesus, who is greater than the one who is in the world, we will triumph over the world through the power and experience of the resurrection (see 1 John 4:4).

The church is an unstoppable force. It is infused with the moving power of God. It is not merely an institution or religious authority. The church must boldly bear witness to the truth about Jesus. When the church abandons falsehood and fearlessly proclaims the truth, its power and purpose will be revitalized. Jesus Christ must be revealed to the world through the church.

# 15

# HAPPINESS COMES WHEN
# WE COME BACK

ॐ

WITHIN THE VAST BIOLOGICAL WORLD of the animal kingdom, one could argue that the most interesting and enigmatic ability some creatures possess is the homing instinct. Salmon, for example, hatch from eggs and swim downriver to live in the vast ocean and after several years swim back thousands of miles upstream to lay eggs where they were born. Bees go far away to find honey and then come back to the hive. Fruit flies are drawn to the earth's magnetic field and pass this ability on to their offspring genetically. It is said that animals like elephants and pigeons return to their homeland toward the end of their lifespans so they might pass at home.

This homing instinct is also inherent in humans. One reason why refugees or immigrants feel lonely during holidays is that they do not or cannot return to their homeland. The Korean word for *passing away* also means *to return*, expressing an understanding that people return somewhere at their deaths. This instinct to return to their homeland is present in people from all nations and walks of life. The human longing for a homeland is a way for God to lead us to our eternal homeland. C. S. Lewis said, "If I find in myself a desire which no experience in this world can satisfy, the most probable explanation is that I was made for another world"—the eternal world. The world we live in is not eternal, and there is an eternal world prepared for us by God. Humans have a homing instinct for the eternal kingdom prepared by God. Therefore, nothing in this world can satisfy that longing.

In a seemingly paradoxical way, embracing our homing instinct toward eternity can allow us to enjoy satisfaction in life as we explore the expanse of human experience. This homing instinct is used as a way to listen to the gospel of Jesus Christ, guiding us even as we live in a sinful and broken world. Jesus' words "My Father's house has many rooms" (John 14:2), "I go and prepare a place" (John 14:3), and "The one who believes in me will live, even though they die" (John 11:25) evoke the homing instinct that God has put in humans and move us forward to the gospel.

Sometimes the land we inhabit shows our spiritual condition. In Old Testament history, the land where the people of Israel stayed showed their spiritual state. Four spiritual and symbolic lands appear in the Bible: Egypt, the Wilderness, Canaan, and Babylon. Egypt was the land of idolatry, a place that did not know God and served the gods of the world. The Wilderness was a land of unbelief and wandering, a place without faith that remained separate from the Promised Land. Canaan represented the spiritual homeland and Babylon was a land of exile—a result of disobedience and punishment.

Spiritually, we live in one of these four lands. When we are in a land that is not in accordance with God's will, God brings us back to our spiritual homeland through suffering. When Jacob lived in Shechem, he encountered great suffering through the incident with his daughter Dinah, and God called him back to his spiritual homeland, Bethel. The call to go back to Bethel was a call to return to Canaan, the spiritual homeland given to their ancestor Abraham, and a command to return to a life that sought the eternal kingdom.

Difficult experiences like the Covid-19 pandemic provide an opportunity to return to our spiritual homeland. We should look back and see if we have been staying in Egypt, the Wilderness, or Babylon—which God does not want. Longing for a physical homeland cannot lead us to happiness. We have to go to our spiritual homeland. We must discover the promised land beyond this earthly realm, the spiritual homeland that leads us to live on this earth until we reach our eternal homeland and stay there. That place may be a far-off foreign country, the mission field, or our physical homeland. The important thing is not where exactly we are but whether we see that place as a spiritual homeland.

# 16

# THE SPIRITUALITY OF SIMPLICITY

❧

WHEN DESCRIBING A PERSON AS "SIMPLE," we may mean one of two things. The first has a negative connotation, that a person lacks depth, judgment, or intelligence. We usually feel frustrated with simple people, when someone does not fully understand a situation yet makes a comment, or when they act impulsively based on scant knowledge. The second meaning is more positive, describing someone who lives their life centered on key values without being swayed by circumstance. Simplicity is a very noble virtue.

The life God asks of his children is a life defined by the latter definition—a life of simplicity but not simplism. *Simplism* is the oversimplification of complex phenomena, in which people reject complexity. *Simplicity*, however, accepts and understands complexity but remains unshaken by it. We need a spirituality of simplicity.

There are two keys to a simple spirituality. The first is to focus less on the external and the second is to focus less on the self. Those who focus on the external, on people and circumstances outside of their control, will inevitably be shaken. Satan likes to attack our spirits with lies, appearing as a blessing on the surface while cursing from within, especially using other people as weapons. Those who crave recognition or overreact to criticism are the most susceptible to these kinds of attacks.

We must also be careful of excessive internal focus. It is dangerous to be intoxicated by external factors, yes, but it is even more dangerous to be intoxicated by the self. Those who struggle with self-satisfaction will find that they are even more easily swayed by the slightest external disturbance.

However, if you look only at God, you will not fall so quickly into suffering. For people who focus on God, suffering disappears like the morning mist that covers the earth and vanishes as the sun rises, covering only the surface of their hearts. If they think more about God than themselves and love God more than their own interests, they can lead a simple life.

A simple soul focuses only on God and firmly cuts off all useless things. Those with simple souls entrust all their worries and fears to God and enjoy inner peace. It is a grace to attain such simplicity. Without the grace of God working within us, it would be impossible. This simplicity is reached through discipline. Richard Foster calls this discipline of simplicity "disciplined grace."

Jesus asserted, "'Love the Lord your God with all your heart and with all your soul and with all your mind.' This is the first and greatest commandment" (Matthew 22:37-38).

Loving God with all your heart is not enough. Love cannot be called love unless it shows itself through will and strength. When you love God with all your heart, life, will, and strength then there will be no division.

The only one worthy of loving with all our heart, life, and will is God himself. When we love only God with everything we have, our divided inner selves become completely integrated. This is the original purpose for which humans were created. Our inner selves are divided because we have deviated from that original purpose. To be completely integrated, we must return to this original purpose and focus.

A simple soul is one that loves God and God alone, with all the whole of the heart, life, and will. A simple soul is happy because happiness is gained when human nature and purpose align. Life becomes a reluctant duty and an inevitable burden when we do not love God with all our hearts. There is no joy in duty and burden. But love turns everything into joy.

We enjoy more wealth, resources, and advanced technology than any previous era. However, the dazzling twenty-first century is more fractured than ever. Even with better living conditions, people still struggle. One could even claim that the earth is suffering more than any previous era.

The change we need is to embrace simplicity. If our souls become ones that love God, we can be at peace even if we find ourselves in suffocating situations. "Look at the birds of the air; they do not sow or reap or store away in barns, and yet your heavenly Father feeds them. Are you not much more valuable than they? . . . See how the flowers of the field grow. . . . Not even Solomon in all his splendor was dressed like one of these" (Matthew 6:26-29).

# 17

# SEEK WISDOM

꙳

SOLOMON'S ATTITUDE IN SEEKING the wisdom of discernment from God teaches us how we, too, should seek wisdom from God. Solomon offered a thousand burnt offerings in Gibeon, which were a sacrifice to God on behalf of the entire kingdom. After that, God appeared to Solomon in a dream and asked, "Ask for whatever you want me to give you" (1 Kings 3:5). God is not someone who gives us gifts because of what he has received. God is moved by the attitude of our hearts, not by the amount of our offerings. God saw what Solomon needed and asked him first.

God knows what we need and comes to fulfill those needs. Sometimes God gives us suffering and pain that we don't want. However, looking back at those circumstances, it often turns out that even those difficult things were part of God's providential plan for giving us what we really needed. Thus, part of true discernment is understanding that God seeks us before we seek him. Discernment is perceiving the presence of God and striving to understand how he is speaking to us in this particular moment.

The fact that God first came to Solomon with a question is vitally important. God did not just say, "I think you need the wisdom of discernment as a king, so I will give it to you," without asking any questions. He asked, "What do you want me to give you?" We must deeply consider the reason why God did this.

If God were to grant you one unconditional wish, what would you ask for? Through Solomon's experience, we can learn the importance of discovering what is truly necessary for ourselves. We ask and pray for many things from God. However, we must reflect on whether what we are asking for is really necessary and important. People who do not realize what they truly need cannot properly ask for it, even if God tells them to ask.

Now, a king is someone who makes important decisions. Solomon asked for the wisdom of discernment he needed as a king (see 1 Kings 3:9). Solomon's plea shows us the attitude our hearts should have to obtain spiritual discernment. That attitude is humility. Humility is an essential condition for gaining the wisdom of discernment. It means looking at oneself honestly with truth. A humble person is honest with themselves.

In contrast, the biggest obstacle to spiritual discernment is pride. Proud people forget the grace God has bestowed on them in the past. They seek the wisdom of discernment ultimately for selfish gain. We must not become such proud individuals. We need to be those who seek the wisdom to discern what God wants for us in our present situation.

Now, we can sometimes confuse ambition with God's vision. Even if we eagerly listen to God's Word, we can still live a deceitful life. Impure desires may be hidden within our zeal. Let's not deceive ourselves. Let us seek God's help by honestly confronting ourselves and acknowledging our weakness and incompetence. God will surely grant us the wisdom of discernment.

# 18

# RELY ON TEAMWORK

ॡ

THE BARNA GROUP ASKED PARTICIPANTS, "What's the most important quality in a leader?" in a 2013 survey titled "Christians on Leadership, Calling and Career." Several categories of answers emerged, with many emphasizing the ability to motivate others and to resolve conflicts. Ultimately, the survey touched on the fact that people had various expectations for their leaders. But is it possible for a leader to meet them all?

If a leader claims to meet every expectation, it would be a grave problem. Such a leader would be extremely arrogant. Leaders who assert their self-importance and qualifications usually seek personal influence and cannot lead well, because they overlook the importance of teamwork. As T. S. Eliot wrote, "Half of the harm that is done in this world is due to people who want to feel important."

Teamwork is built on the understanding that every member of the community holds significance. Therefore, a genuine and good leader should make those within their community feel important without pretending to be self-important. There is a saying in Korean: "If you want light, you have to burn all the candles." Your own candle alone cannot sustain the light for a long duration. By sharing your light with others, the flame will never fade. Max De Pree, former president of the furniture company Herman

Miller, wrote in his book *Leadership Is an Art* that leadership is not measured solely by intellectual qualifications but by the atmosphere one creates. Good leaders lead their followers to fulfill their respective and vital roles. Outstanding leadership is revealed in those who follow.

The truth about teamwork becomes even clearer when we observe the animal kingdom. When a flock of wild geese migrates, they fly in a V-shaped formation. The lead goose takes the brunt of the effort, but when it becomes tired, it falls back and another takes its place. If a goose falls sick or gets injured and lags behind, two others leave the formation and remain by its side until it recovers and can rejoin the flock.

To achieve effective teamwork, not only the leader but also those who stand alongside the leader play crucial roles. Secondary leadership, in particular, holds significant influence. Musician Leonard Bernstein remarked that the most difficult instrument to play in an orchestra is the "second fiddle." Second violinists who play with as much passion as the first violinists are rare but extremely vital.

One of the most beautiful examples of secondary leadership in the Bible can be found in Caleb. He was among the spies sent to explore the land of Canaan alongside Joshua. Of the twelve spies, only Joshua and Caleb reported back because of their faith. This allowed them and their descendants to enter the Promised Land after forty years of wandering in the wilderness. Caleb lived a hidden life behind the scenes for over four decades. Yet he never asserted his rights over Joshua. At the age of eighty-five, when Joshua distributed the lands of Canaan, Caleb volunteered to conquer the challenging Hebron Mountains. Caleb was the second-in-command in Israel, and no one would have contested it if he had requested the largest plot of the most fertile land.

However, in his later years, Caleb chose to assist Joshua by selecting the most demanding region.

Teamwork thrives when there are exceptional collaborators beside the leader. As Ecclesiastes 4:9 tells us, "Two are better than one, because they have a good return for their labor." The essence of teamwork lies in acknowledging that two heads are better than one. We cannot achieve everything on our own. A team always surpasses the capabilities of one individual. There is a saying that a team's IQ is always higher than the sum of its individuals. Psychological studies reveal that group decision-making consistently yields better results than individual decision-making. If one rope can withstand 40 pounds of force, three ropes tied together can withstand not just 120 pounds but can actually withstand more than 200 pounds due to the effect of synergy. If inanimate objects can benefit from synergy, imagine the tremendous effect it can have when humans, created in the image of God, cooperate with one another.

We hope and pray for leaders who will exemplify this kind of leadership. We desire a leader who proclaims, "We did it together!" rather than a self-important one who claims, "I did it myself."

# 19

# NOT THE AUTHORITY
# BUT A STEWARD

THE QUESTION OF AUTHORITY is an important issue in an era of religious pluralism. During the eighteenth century, the Enlightenment swept through Western cultures, advocating for autonomy, self-consciousness, and the disregard of traditional authorities. Reason and conscience became the guiding lights of culture and sacred authority was subjected to questioning.

Since the Enlightenment, science has ascended to a position of tremendous authority. As such, those who question established scientific facts are often marginalized and deemed unenlightened. But how does this principle extend to matters of faith?

People readily accept the authority of science while dismissing the authority of the Bible and in turn denying the authority of God. Man-made false authorities have thus eclipsed the authority of God.

Yet when God created all things, he established an invisible authority over them (see Colossians 1:15-16). This authority is good and holy, an authority that we should submit to. It is an honor to represent his authority, but this also carries a great danger of misrepresenting his authority—especially to God! Sadly, such risks have become a reality as humanity has succumbed to a spiritual authority that betrays God (see Ephesians 6:12), denying his rightful authority.

During Jesus' ministry on earth, one word continually emerged in people's questions and astonishment: authority. "By what *authority* does he do these things?" (see Mark 11:28; also Mark 4:35-41). The religious scholars were amazed by the *authority* of Jesus' teachings.

In the wilderness, when Jesus was tempted by Satan, he confronted the authority of the world. Satan offered Jesus all authority and glory if only he would bow down before him. Yet Jesus rejected this corrupt and worldly authority.

Jesus operated under the authority of God. He did not exalt himself but wielded the authority bestowed on him by God. Jesus demonstrated three key aspects of authority.

First, Jesus made it clear that his authority was not self-derived but came from God (see John 5:30). He functioned as a steward of authority, recognizing that even the words he spoke were given by God (see John 7:16).

Second, Jesus refused to claim glory for himself, even while exercising his authority (see John 7:18). In contrast, the corrupt authority of the world compels individuals to exalt themselves. Satan tempted Adam and Eve with the lie that they would have an authority equal to that of God.

Third, Jesus used his authority to serve and help others. He was a man of authority, using his power to meet the needs of those around him. In contrast, worldly authority seeks to accumulate power at the expense of others, resulting in authoritarianism. Consequently, the world is replete with individuals possessing authority but lacking true influence.

Jesus did not rely on the authority of the world as a display of power. Instead, he served as a steward of authority, even to the cross. His authority posed a threat to worldly authorities, and he courageously criticized the leaders who coveted power and status in the temple. Jesus served as an example by not succumbing to the world's authority.

As we consider reforms within the church, one fundamental and primary task emerges: pastors must relinquish their power and their authority. They are to live as stewards of the authority bestowed on them, just as they are stewards of their time, talents, and treasures.

Jesus used the image of a child to illustrate this lowering of oneself (see Matthew 18:1-4). He did not speak of imitating the immaturity of a child but highlighted the humble attitude of children toward authority. Children are unfamiliar with using power. They do not know how to use worldly authority. Therefore, the call is to become childlike witnesses of the kingdom of God as faithful stewards of authority. If church leaders can steward God's authority rather than their own, the church will bear much fruit.

# YOUR BEST MAY NOT BE GOD'S BEST

THE ULTIMATE ACHIEVEMENT FOR A LEADER is not personal *success* but *succession*. It is the leader's final task to pass on their vision to the next leader and gracefully withdraw so that God's ministry can endure.

Undoubtedly, receiving credit for one's work and receiving a fair evaluation is important. Great leaders are those who usually possess many achievements. However, if the greatest leaders fail to bequeath their vision and their ministry to the next generation of leaders, the fruit of their labors—built through tears—can disintegrate in an instant.

Leaders who falter in their final duties struggle with the temptation to prioritize personal legacy over a selfless surrender. They become reluctant to relinquish the office that once offered them praise and reverence. Before that final moment, they humbly follow God's will. But their attitude seems to shift when the time for them to move on comes. They suddenly seek recognition for their merits and may even blame their successor for wanting to undermine them. Such actions obscure God's glory. Oswald Chambers profoundly asserted that the moment no one can recognize you is the time you've reached the highest of heights, for then you are rightly committed to Jesus Christ. People should not see your abilities and attribute them to you. They should see only God's ability revealed through you.

Let us look at Moses, for instance. He pleaded with God to allow him to set foot in the Promised Land of Canaan. This seemed like a reasonable reward, considering the arduous journey of faithfully leading the Israelites during the exodus and through forty years of wilderness wanderings. However, God flatly refused. While appearing merciless, God desired for Moses to end his life not as a *great* leader who led the Israelites out of slavery and into the Promised Land but as a *good* leader who was humble and obedient.

The story of Moses' end reminds us that we will never be able to grasp the whole picture. Only God possesses that vantage point while we can only perceive a fraction of it. Consequently, what we ask for may not always be the best. It may seem optimal from our limited perspective, but God's viewpoint differs. In truth, Moses could not have imagined anything more marvelous than entering the land of Canaan. Yet God had something even more wondrous in mind.

God intended to display his holiness through Moses by prohibiting him from entering Canaan. The decision was already made when Moses, provoked by the people's sins, struck the rock with his staff (see Numbers 20). Through this act, God unequivocally demonstrated that the sin of a leader is never taken lightly and that God's people must remember his holiness.

God also revealed his greatness through this act. In the ancient world, ancestral worship was prevalent. If Moses had entered Canaan and then died, there would have been the danger of the people deifying him and treating him like an idol. God prevented Moses from becoming more important to the Israelites than himself. Greatness can be perilous. No servant of God can ever be in a position higher than God.

Moses believed in the greatness of God. He trusted that even though he would not lead the Israelites into Canaan, God would undoubtedly fulfill his promise through someone else. A leader should wholly and fully trust in God. We must have faith that God can manifest his greatness through someone far less significant than us.

Martin Luther King Jr. (1929–1968) echoed these sentiments, alluding to Moses' experience in a speech he delivered in Memphis:

> Like anybody, I would like to live a long life—longevity has its place. But I'm not concerned about that now. I just want to do God's will. And he's allowed me to go up to the mountain. And I've looked over, and I've seen the promised land. I may not get there with you. But I want you to know tonight, that we, as a people, will get to the promised land. And so I'm happy tonight; I'm not worried about anything; I'm not fearing any man. Mine eyes have seen the glory of the coming of the Lord.

Those who live according to God's will find joy in merely glimpsing the promised land. Whether or not we can set foot on that land becomes inconsequential. What truly matters is understanding the extent of God's will. If God's will aligns with what we perceive, that alone will bring us happiness. And we will find true joy in wholeheartedly supporting those who will succeed us and witnessing God's will fulfilled through them. That is the mark of a genuine servant of God. It means being utilized by God as a good leader, surpassing mere greatness. The church desperately needs these types of good leaders.

## PART THREE

# CHOOSE TRUTH, EVEN WHEN IT'S PAINFUL

# MAKING THE RIGHT DECISIONS

WHEN MAKING DECISIONS, individuals often rely on criteria they deem right according to their own understanding. However, they often fail to critically examine the rationality of these criteria. This lack of scrutiny is one of the reasons behind the perpetual controversies and disputes that plague our society. The differences in criteria and the failure to understand the perspectives of others only perpetuate confrontations.

Criteria for decisions can be classified into three categories. The first category is *truth*, which serves as an absolute and universally applicable standard. Truth transcends time and holds authority over all people. Yet the postmodern worldview argues that there is no absolute truth for everyone to accept. According to this view, scientific truth is the only public truth, while moral truth is relative. This perspective discourages making truth claims unless they are scientifically verified. It often elevates tolerance and acceptance as absolute truths.

The problem with this idea is that the proposition itself, "There is no absolute truth," is framed as an absolute truth. This contradiction is rather absurd. Despite the prevailing notions of this age rejecting absolute truth, truth itself remains alive. Just as evil is a tangible reality, goodness exists as a moral reality that is always right. Therefore, goodness is truth. Those who believe in the existence of goodness should also acknowledge the existence of absolute truth, which applies to all of us. This absolute truth serves as the most crucial criterion for decision-making.

The second category is *values*. Values are not inherently right or wrong; they are relative criteria shaped by the culture of a community. They can evolve with time, and what holds authority in one community may not do so in another. Values emerge naturally within a community as time progresses and are often referred to as "doctrine." Although the world may have become a global village, with a homogenizing culture through social media, each country and ethnicity still adheres to slightly differing values. Attempting to impose the values of one community onto another can lead to significant conflicts. Therefore, values must undergo rigorous scrutiny to acquire the authority of truth. The reason we accept the Bible as truth is not merely that it was accepted by communities in a specific era but that it has transcended culture and withstood the test of time and scrutiny.

The third category is *preference*. Preferences can be arbitrary and are based on personal criteria. They are typically applied to mundane choices that do not necessitate community consensus. Distinguishing between preferences is generally less ambiguous compared to distinguishing between truth and values.

The ideal decision-making process encompasses the adherence to absolute truth, respect for community values, and the consideration of individual preferences. However, it is often challenging to satisfy all three aspects simultaneously. Furthermore, the problem is exacerbated when the importance of these criteria is inverted in times of adversity. Preferences take precedence, with values only minimally considered and truth disregarded. This phenomenon is succinctly captured in the phrase "everyone did what was right in their own eyes," describing an era of spiritual darkness, the biblical age of the judges. The phrase portrays a society where even the values upheld by previous generations are abandoned.

An evil leader prioritizes personal preferences over community values, often elevating them above absolute truth. This pattern is exemplified by the Nazi regime in Germany and can be observed in the current regime of North Korea. On the other hand, a good leader willingly sets aside personal preferences and respects the values of the community. Moreover, good leaders lead the community toward values that align with absolute truth. Truth and goodness should be the moral compass of any leader. Greed and ambition will lead leaders astray. Dorothy Sayers (1893–1957), a British detective fiction writer and Christian philosopher, noted in her book *Letters to a Diminished Church* that there are two reasons why people fall into the sin of lust. One is the result of primal instincts, while the other arises from philosophical bankruptcy. Sayers considered "moral laxity" and the state of philosophical ruin to be the more significant factor. When a person feels weary and unsatisfied, they often turn to lust in search of stimulation. However, the more perilous issue lies in the moral decline accompanying lust, which can be remedied only by addressing its underlying causes.

Instead of merely addressing the symptoms, we must treat the cause and save our society from the bankruptcy of philosophy. We need to engage in thoughtful introspection regarding the criteria we establish. In a state of philosophical bankruptcy, truth and values become indistinguishable from personal preferences. Present-day Korean society is experiencing the harsh consequences of such bankruptcy. Leaders easily overlook values and truth, prioritizing their own preferences and making them the absolute standard, particularly when public sentiment aligns with their preferences. However, the ideal of liberal democracy, which we must never abandon, is to respect one another's preferences while prioritizing community values and striving to become a society where truth holds the highest authority.

# 22

# THE RIGHT MENTALITY

PEOPLE HEAR ONLY WHAT THEY WANT TO HEAR and see only what they want to see. It is no wonder that we can't see and hear all things. This is because there are limitations to cognitive ability.

Additionally, people possess different desires, experiences, and personal characteristics that further contribute to selective perception. Takeshi Yoro, an emeritus professor at the Medical College of Tokyo University, aptly referred to this phenomenon as a "wall of fools" in his book *Baka no Kabe* (literally, *The Wall of Fools*).

The Gospel of John also illustrates this phenomenon of selective perception. When God the Father's voice was heard by Jesus, some interpreted it as thunder, while others believed an angel had spoken to Jesus (see John 12:28-29). Although they heard the same voice, their interpretations differed because they perceived the sound according to their past memories and biases, selectively choosing and interpreting the information.

Jesus indicated that people's inability to understand his words stemmed from their inability to truly hear. He said, "Why is my language not clear to you? Because you are unable to hear what I say" (John 8:43). In this context, "not being able to hear" does not refer to physical hearing but rather to the obstructions caused by prejudices, stereotypes, and worldviews that hindered their comprehension of Jesus' message.

How we hear and what we hear vary depending on our individual personalities. Our instinctive and selective listening shapes what we hold in our minds and what we seek to obtain from the information. Therefore, Jesus advised, "Consider carefully what you hear" (Mark 4:24) and "Consider carefully how you listen" (Luke 8:18).

Consequently, our manner of listening and what we choose to hear reveal our identity. What we hear reflects who we are. Rash judgments about others may actually be judgments about ourselves. When we listen, we do so with hidden biases and emotions, such as love, hatred, prejudice, stereotypes, grudges, and disgust. Those who live shallow lives will interpret Jesus' words in a shallow manner, while those who live noble lives will listen in a noble way.

Many people base their arguments on different types of logic, but ultimately it is their own mind that influences and guides their logic. Social discord and prejudice arise when the psychology of the self surpasses and undermines logic. Conversely, socioemotional maturity follows rational wisdom after individuals set aside their preconceived notions and objectively examine the evidence.

Even in Christian life and within church communities, there are instances where psychology and preference outweigh logic. Some disregard the logical revelations found in the Word of God and selectively choose to believe only what aligns with their personal desires. They interpret the logic of the Bible to fit their own beliefs.

True obedience entails humbling oneself before the logic of God's Word. Faith relies not on one's own mindset but on the logic derived from objective facts. Faith is not self-confidence but trust in God through confidence in the evidence provided by God.

The maturity of a church community depends on its ability to objectively scrutinize the judgments of its members. It depends on following the logic of God's Word and the logic of objective evidence rather than succumbing to personal biases. This depends on one's willingness to listen not only to what one wants to hear but also to what one may dislike. In any society, true reform occurs when the dominance of psychology over logic is relinquished.

Do we only approach those who speak words we agree with, or do we genuinely respect and draw close to those who speak words we dislike hearing? Regardless of culture and society, reform occurs when an egocentric mentality makes way for logic.

# 23

# WHY DO HUMANS WANT TO BE GODS?

A GROWING NUMBER OF PEOPLE are trying to become gods. This trend has accelerated as material civilization and scientific technology have advanced. In 2021, one of the world's richest celebrities succeeded in a space flight that exceeded an altitude of sixty-two miles. The development of the space industry to solve some of humanity's problems is worth celebrating, but it is not a matter of pride to consider oneself great by merely going high up in the sky with enormous amounts of money. It is a matter of how we see ourselves and how we see God.

More frightening than the handful of people trying to prove their greatness through technological advances or with wealth and power is the category of people who try to become gods by becoming the standard of norms themselves. These people reject any objective criteria given from outside. They even reject the biological gender they are born with and demand recognition for the "social gender" they choose themselves. Influential humanities scholars encourage people to be true to themselves and listen to their inner voice. They argue that individual feelings are the ultimate source of authority and that good and evil are determined by how each person feels. For them, what they feel is good is good, and what they feel is bad is evil. This era, more than ever, sanctifies each individual's subjective feelings.

Yuval Noah Harari, a bestselling author and a professor of history at Hebrew University, is a thorough evolutionist who laid out various antibiblical hypotheses based on evolution in his book *Sapiens*. It is a regrettable reality that such arguments have become a global bestseller. However, in the concluding section, he makes a meaningful observation that a fundamental transformation is taking place in human consciousness and identity.

Moreover, despite the astonishing things that humans are capable of doing, we remain unsure of our goals and we seem to be as discontented as ever. We have advanced from canoes to galleys to steamships to space shuttles – but nobody knows where we're going. We are more powerful than ever before, but have very little idea what to do with all that power. Worse still, humans seem to be more irresponsible than ever. Self-made gods with only the laws of physics to keep us company, we are accountable to no one. We are consequently wreaking havoc on our fellow animals and on the surrounding ecosystem, seeking little more than our own comfort and amusement, yet never finding satisfaction.

Is there anything more dangerous than dissatisfied and irresponsible gods who don't know what they want?

Even radical evolutionists criticize the fact that humans are trying to become gods. People are breaking down the order and limits bestowed on humans by considering themselves as gods. They can build a machine to fly into space, but they don't know where they are actually heading. Despite the tremendous advances in science and technology, they are not reducing the pain in the world but are instead plunging it into greater suffering.

Why are people becoming so dangerous? They do not feel any responsibility for their actions as they try to become gods, which only exacerbates their pain. It is because they have abandoned their Creator God. It is because they are destroying the created order and undermining bioethics. The fundamental crisis of humanity originated from the virus of sin, which depends on oneself rather than God. The people who try to become gods themselves include not only those who boast great achievements but also those who try to resolve their longing using their own methods.

However, all their efforts to become gods themselves prove only that humans cannot live without God and that humanity needs God. They try to fill the void left by leaving the Creator God. This is not only impossible but also a path to more unhappiness. May people realize that the true way to live lies in letting God be God in their lives.

# 24

# TRUTHS EVERYONE MUST ACCEPT

৵

THIS ERA IS BEHOLDEN to one contradictory maxim: "There is no absolute truth that everyone must accept." This implies that something becomes true only when an individual accepts it as truth. Individuals decide the truthfulness according to their interpretations and feelings. Turning truth into something relative ultimately degrades truth to the level of values.

Values can differ depending on continent and ethnicity, even within one country, depending on regions. Values are relative and change according to how communities perceive them. Therefore, everyone must respect the values that others deem important.

However, truth is different. Truth must apply to all times and all people. The reason we can call scientifically verified facts "truth" is that they apply consistently throughout time. Those who study and research science must unconditionally accept scientific truth, regardless of their choices. It is impossible to selectively accept scientific truth as a relative value depending on changes in time.

The problem of this era is that it denies the existence of an absolute truth and claims that relative values are truth. Historically, many things were accepted as absolute truth, not only scientific truth but also moral truth. Examples include "True love involves sacrifice," "Forgiveness frees each other," and "The arrogant will be destroyed." These truths reside in people's hearts and can be more clearly found in the Bible.

The Bible is a book of truth given by God, the source of absolute truth. Amazingly, many truths recently discovered in science also appear in the Bible, which is not a science book. Above all, the morality stated in the Bible is an absolute truth. It is not only summarized in the Ten Commandments but also evidenced throughout biblical history. Many people argue that the Bible, being an ancient book, should be reevaluated in relative-value terms to fit today's culture. Of course, when reading or analyzing the Bible, it should be interpreted and applied by taking into account the cultural elements of the time it was recorded. However, the morality of the Bible goes beyond culture as an absolute truth. This truth is clear and does not change depending on individual interpretations and feelings.

At the center of this is the order by which God created humans as male and female. The gender distinction between male and female is not only a truth found in the Bible but also common sense proven through science and history. How should we accept the argument that this gender distinction is not a truth that everyone must embrace? Is it not a tremendous contradiction to claim that gender is a value that individuals can pick and choose? In this era, Christians must start by sharing the rather obvious news that there is truth that everyone must accept.

# 25

# FINDING YOUR PLACE IN
# LIFE DURING DISASTER

᪥

DURING PAINFUL TIMES we experience and understand the authority of God. God works not *in spite of* but *through* suffering. Without suffering we would not change easily, so God has no choice but to use suffering.

One way God uses suffering is by answering our prayers and quickly removing the painful circumstances. God rejoices when we rejoice and does not want us to suffer needlessly. There are times, however, when God has a purpose in allowing suffering to occur for our sake.

Many times God molds our inner selves through the pain so that we might find our rightful place. We may think that the pain we face in life makes our lives a mess. It can seem even more painful because we feel that our pain prevents us from being in the place we ought to be—spiritually, emotionally, physically, and even vocationally. However, God can lead us to the right place through suffering. Pain has an amazing ability to reveal what is hidden within us, such as where we place our life's purpose, what values we pursue, and especially what kind of relationship we have with God. Pain helps us realize that a situation we thought was normal could be abnormal, and a situation we thought was abnormal could be the right path to return to normalcy.

We need a perspective on the pandemic that views it as the second way God deals with suffering. One thing is certain: God has given us a time of pause to prepare for the final end times. To pray, we must stop. To readjust our direction, we must slow down.

The pandemic led to something that no developed country or international organization could have done. Carbon dioxide emissions decreased, and animals that were on the brink of extinction began reappearing. While the things we were used to fell apart in this enforced pseudo-sabbatical, the things we lost began returning.

The purpose for suffering is for us to find the right place in life. Pain makes us think about things we never thought about and doubt things we thought were securely in place within us.

There is a famous story about Albert Einstein. Once, he lost his ticket while traveling by train. The conductor came to check the ticket, but Einstein was preoccupied trying to find it. The conductor, who recognized him, said, "Doctor, I know who you are. I am confident that you have bought a ticket, so don't worry. It's fine."

And he walked away. But a moment later the conductor looked back and saw Einstein still searching for the ticket under the seat.

He returned and said, "Dr. Einstein, you don't have to worry. I know who you are."

Einstein then looked up and replied, "I know who I am too. The problem is, I don't know where I am going."

The destination is important in life. We think we have to decide our life's destination and path for ourselves, and that usually is a path without suffering or struggle. But that is not a Christian path. Pain is a sign from God to repent and reset our lives from our sin. It is a sign from God to change direction from a self-centered life where we determine our destination ourselves to a life looking toward the destination God has set.

Moreover, pain is a tool that leads us to a deserving place to receive prepared blessings. Pain itself is not a blessing. Pain is merely suffering. But beyond the pain there are blessings that God has prepared waiting for us. When we know this, we truly welcome pain and the blessings beyond it with gratitude.

There is an anecdote about the pastor of a small church in the Midwest. One time, he visited a church member's house and saw two large jars filled with marbles on the shelf. One jar was full of marbles, while the other had only a few. He asked what the jars were for and why the marbles were there. The church member replied, "Throughout my life, I have experienced God turning many burdens of life into blessings. The jar with only a few marbles represents the burdens in my life. Originally, that jar was full of marbles. But every time God turned my burden into a blessing, I moved a marble from the jar of burdens to the jar of blessings. Now the jar of blessings is full, and there are only a few burdens left. Complaining in times of suffering is not helpful, I realized, and seeking the hand of God that changes the world is what truly helps during dark times."

In a world full of suffering, we hear not only the cries of pain but also the living voice of God leading us back to our rightful place. I hope that no matter what pain comes our way, we can firmly orient our souls in the right direction.

# 26

# THE KEY IS ALWAYS THE GOSPEL

BEFORE WE KNEW IT, we became familiar with the phrase "socially distant." Of course, the trend away from face-to-face socialization is not solely due to the Covid-19 pandemic. It was already a major trend of our time with the onset of social media, and rapidly accelerated because of the pandemic.

The greatest danger of a socially distant society is the severing of genuine interpersonal relationships, especially as people depend more on media that pollutes the soul. In the meantime, the separation between the church and the world has progressed, and even Christians have come to view faith and life as different entities. The truth they know well in their heads does not appear in their hearts.

The Pharisees were people who fell into this trap in the time of Jesus. During antiquity, the Pharisees considered themselves separate from others and sought social superiority by claiming they were righteous before God. They institutionalized fasting by fasting twice a week; however, the more they fasted, the more arrogant their hearts became. The more arrogant they became, the more distant they were from God. Initially, they created a system of traditions for the sake of the soul, but over time it became a system of traditions to satisfy the desires of the flesh.

The pandemic challenged Christians to define the essence of a church. If we equate our own religious traditions with faith, like the Pharisees at the time of Jesus, then we need to throw them all away. If we are keeping certain church systems and traditions to nurture our pride instead of our souls, then these must be stripped away. Through the pandemic we learned an important lesson: *it's not enough just to go to church; we must become the church.*

The following words of John Havlik are important to remember:

The church is never a place, but always a people; never a fold but always a flock; never a sacred building but always a believing assembly. The church is you who pray, not where you pray. A structure of brick or marble can no more be the church than your clothes of serge or satin can be you. There is in this world nothing sacred but man, no sanctuary of man but the soul.

People who attend church have prioritized the importance of their physical location within the church building. However, a true Christian knows that being in the presence of Christ is more important. The vitality of the church is manifested through experiencing the presence of Jesus Christ.

From now on, as life now shifts into a post-pandemic era, the true essence and power of the church must be realized and Christians must return to the basics: facing Christ and experiencing his presence. The religious traditions might push us to further separate from this world we consider polluted and impure. However, the gospel does not mandate that we separate from the world but that we act as salt and light.

# 27

# TRUTH CANNOT BE DIVIDED
# INTO PUBLIC AND PRIVATE

TRADITIONALLY, THE EASIEST WAY to ethically deal with issues at the institutional level is to differentiate private and public spheres. This differentiation ranges from prohibiting the use of the public budget and labor force for private purposes to prioritizing the interests of the majority over personal interests. By distinguishing between public and private matters, an ethical system is established. Such distinction is absolutely necessary for running a country and its institutions.

However, in modern times there are cases where the distinction between public and private matters has been misused. The most representative example is the division of truth into public and private realms. In the public domain, only truths that can be scientifically verified are accepted, while Christian faith and personal beliefs are relegated to the realm of private truths. Even in countries with a Christian history like the United States, public schools forbid prayer gatherings and Bible readings, and religious events have been excluded from all public institutions. Even saying phrases like "Merry Christmas" has been discouraged in many cases.

What this era is forgetting is that truth cannot be divided into public and private sectors. Truth must be accepted in all areas and recognized as authoritative in any domain. But this day and age blindly accepts each individual's feelings and opinions as if they were the absolute authority of truth, while pushing genuine, objective, and absolute truth to the background. The inclusion of nonbinary in the definitions of gender within antidiscrimination and equality laws forces the recognition of personal and subjective judgments and feelings as truth into the public domain. The scientific objectivity of biological sex is now viewed as a feeling that individuals can choose as they please. Even private schools that were established with the purpose of integrating education with Christian philosophies have begun to prohibit the teaching and spreading of Christianity. Fundamentally, these institutions are regarded as part of the public domain before they are considered Christian private schools.

Abraham Kuyper, a neo-Calvinist scholar and former prime minister of the Netherlands, was the first to develop the concept of sphere sovereignty. According to this concept, each sphere operates independently within its God-given boundaries, and no single sphere should infringe on the proper jurisdiction of another. For the public domain to guarantee public interest, it cannot encroach on private spheres. The public domain's public nature is achieved by respecting the freedom of the private domain to the greatest extent possible. However, our current society needs to understand that wisdom should not succumb to the trap of dividing public and private so irrevocably.

# 28

# LIVES ARE MORE IMPORTANT THAN RIGHTS

ON JUNE 24, 2022, the US Supreme Court overturned a ruling that has guaranteed women's abortion rights since 1973, allowing state governments to independently determine the existence of abortion rights. Conservative states with a majority of Republican supporters, such as Texas and Louisiana, welcomed the decision, while Democratic states, such as New York and California, strongly opposed it. The controversy over abortion and its subsequent cultural war has accelerated divisions within American society.

According to the *New York Times*, immediately after the Supreme Court ruling, states such as Missouri, Arkansas, and Oklahoma banned abortion by state law. It is said that more than half of the US states have already adopted or plan to adopt such measures, highlighting the possibility that abortion might effectively disappear from the entire country. This decision has led to large-scale protests and political divisions.

Did federal judges make their decision without anticipating such division? Certainly not. They likely foresaw the extreme divisions and confrontations but decided to push forward to protect the identity of the United States and avert the wrong course with firm determination. This is not merely because they were Republican supporters; rather, they felt an urgent sense of duty to realign American ethics and culture.

The movie *Unplanned* is based on the true story of a woman named Abby who worked for the largest abortion clinic in the United States. In the movie, Abby witnesses an abortion for the first time in her life and is deeply shocked. She realizes that she has been complicit in killing countless people and, as a result, works to reverse the steps of those seeking abortions, eventually closing an abortion facility. The strong opposition between those trying to protect the lives of fetuses and those leaving the decision to adults themselves is a clear manifestation of a spiritual war that will only intensify in the future.

South Korea has experienced a legal vacuum regarding abortion after the Constitutional Court ruled that the restrictions on abortions were unconstitutional. South Korea must ensure that legislation proceeds in the direction of protecting life so that it does not suffer from the pain of repeating decades of mistakes like the United States. Before any superficial stance in favor or opposition of any system, there must first be a biblically sound understanding of the value of life. Christians must first awaken and pray.

The correct establishment of values concerning life can only be achieved through the church. Church leaders must learn from the abortion debate in the United States and actively lead their communities toward a culture that respects life.

# 29

# TRUTH WITH A GENTLE EMBRACE

I plead with Euodia and I plead with Syntyche to be of the same mind in the Lord. (Philippians 4:2)

Euodia and Syntyche, prominent leaders in the church at Philippi, were embroiled in conflict. Paul directly addresses them, pleading for their hearts to be united. The fact that their names are mentioned in this widely read letter is a reproach and a call to reconciliation for both individuals.

Conflicts in human relationships cause believers to lose the joy found in the Lord, for the joy bestowed by the Lord is experienced within right and peaceful relationships. Moreover, just as a small fire can grow into a raging inferno, a tiny spark of conflict can spread and ultimately devastate an entire community. A community must not overlook small conflicts. Even the smallest seed of discord must be handled and resolved with utmost care. Ideally, conflicts will be preempted and prevented from arising altogether.

However, conflicts do arise in the church. Because the church is a gathering of diverse people, conflict is unavoidable. The church should be a community that skillfully resolves problems in a healthy manner. In his book *The Different Drum*, M. Scott Peck observes,

> The Church likes to refer to itself as the "Body of Christ." But it behaves as if it thought it could be the Body of Christ

painlessly, as if it could be the Body without having to be stretched, almost torn apart, as if it could be the Body of Christ without having to carry its own cross, without having to hang up on that cross in the agony of conflict. In thinking that it could be thus painlessly the Church has made a lie out of the expression the "Body of Christ."

As Peck points out, a true church community should be capable of being stretched. Just as each individual must embrace a life of risk to be a genuine Christian, the church as a whole must be willing to take risks to become the body of Christ. Yet why does the church not demand commitment from its members? According to Peck, fear is the answer. He suggests that the church should even conduct a roll call every Sunday, signifying the extent of commitment expected. Nevertheless, he argues that the church refrains from such demanding attendance not because of a lack of expectations but out of fear.

"Let your gentleness be evident to all. The Lord is near" (Philippians 4:5). Gentleness here signifies more than mere acceptance; it does not imply letting things slide without conditions, ignoring the truth. True gentleness entails firmly upholding the truth and dealing with it reasonably. It involves overcoming conflicts, trusting that the Lord, who is near to us, will ultimately judge all things. Recognizing ourselves as pilgrims and travelers and acknowledging that the Lord is the judge, not us, we relinquish control and entrust everything to the Lord, rather than presuming that everything depends on us.

When the church extends its embrace to someone, it should do so to foster genuine community, not merely to increase congregational numbers. Regrettably, the church has embraced people out of greed rather than out of love. Miroslav Volf, a professor at Yale

University, explains the profound connection between exclusion and embrace in one of his theological publications. He asserts that there can be no truth without a willingness to embrace others and be embraced by others, and there can be no embrace without a commitment to truth.

In a situation of conflict, desiring justice alone is insufficient; we require something greater than justice. We must desire to embrace and to be embraced. Justice cannot exist without a willingness to embrace, and without justice, there can be no truly enduring embrace.

Truth exists for the sake of love. God allows people to experience pain in order to heal them with love. Genuine truth incorporates a willingness to embrace truth with love.

# 30

# TRUE AUTHORITY LEADS
# TO TRUE FREEDOM

THERE IS A CRITERION FOR EVALUATING whether someone's authority is genuine or not. It depends on whether they
guarantee freedom for those who follow them. Authority that
does not guarantee freedom is power and tyranny. True authority,
however, ensures genuine freedom, just as God's authority was
true when he created humans as free beings.

Modern people resist and deny authority because of the
wounds they've experienced from losing their freedom under
false authorities. Christians' inability to submit to authority
and their fear and doubt stem from a misunderstanding of authority. Obedience to Christ does not annihilate our individu-
ality and will, but rather fosters personal growth and enriches
our free will.

People believe they are thinking freely on their own. However,
their thoughts are not free but bound by something. They are tied
to opposing views and claims that exalt themselves against the
knowledge of God. These claims have become Satan's stronghold,
imprisoning people. These entanglements exist in the form of
ideas and worldviews across different eras and cultures. Even
though people seem to think freely, they are actually believing
false and lofty claims that go against the knowledge of God.

A person's thoughts and life can only be free under one authority—the authority of truth. If one's thoughts are based on falsehood, one cannot be free. Many of our thoughts are false, and we are not enjoying freedom because we are immersed in delusions and errors.

Jesus wants to place our thoughts under his authority. "You will know the truth, and the truth will set you free" (John 8:32). For humans, true freedom is living according to our created purpose. As God's creations, we can be free only by obeying and living under our Creator. No one is born truly free. For a certain period, we are dependent on a mother's embrace for survival. We must learn and understand freedom within the confinements of rules and limitations.

Although people appear to be free when they become adults, they never truly experience freedom. Dependency on parents is replaced by dependency on others. An overattachment to a mother can turn into addictions of various natures—alcohol, drugs, gambling, or even sexual addictions. People lose their freedom and become trapped by their own whims because they reject the One who grants them true freedom—the Creator God. Rejecting the fact that humans should love, obey, and live in accordance with God is mistaken as freedom, but without God, we are not truly free.

To enjoy the freedom of true knowledge, we must realize the words given by the apostle Paul: "The weapons we fight with are not the weapons of the world. On the contrary, they have divine power to demolish strongholds. We demolish arguments and every pretension that sets itself up against the knowledge of God, and we take captive every thought to make it obedient to Christ" (2 Corinthians 10:4-5).

Only by fully acknowledging the authority of Christ, denying oneself, and following Christ can one live the freest life. A life fully devoted to Christ is the freest life. Confessing that one can do nothing without Christ, one becomes able to do all things in Jesus. Just as a musician performing according to a score is not confined by the composition but rather expressing true freedom, one who lives fully in Christ is truly free.

Recognize the authority of Christ and submit all claims and thoughts under Christ's authority. Then you can enjoy true knowledge and freedom.

## PART FOUR

# DENY YOURSELF AND TAKE UP YOUR CROSS

# 31

# HAVE YOU LOST YOUR HUMILITY?

࿔

THROUGHOUT MY CAREER AS A PASTOR, people often ask me: "What is the greatest challenge in ministry?" Whenever I'm asked this, my response comes without hesitation: "It's me."

You might wonder if I'm feigning humility, but I assure you it is the truth. The stumbling blocks in my pastoral journey are not challenging circumstances or disobedient congregants. It is me. It is the pastor. More precisely, difficulties in ministry almost always arise when a pastor has lost humility. I believe that all the problems a pastor encounters in ministry can be traced back to the pastor's pride.

Pride is an ailment that provides pleasure solely to the one who is prideful. Humility, moreover, is not the absence of pride; it is the awareness that pride resides within oneself. Humility is acknowledging that we cannot truly live unless we completely deny ourselves and set aside our pride.

C. S. Lewis, in his book *Mere Christianity*, describes pride in the following way: "According to Christian teachers, the essential vice, the utmost evil, is pride. Unchastity, anger, greed, drunkenness, and all that, are mere flea bites in comparison: it was through pride that the devil became the devil: Pride leads to every other vice: it is the complete anti-God state of mind."

Meanwhile, Andrew Murray stated, "Humility is the path to death, because in death humility gives the highest proof of its perfection. Humility is the blossom of which death to self is the perfect fruit."

The essence of humility is recognizing and experiencing the death of one's old self. Humility leads us to die to ourselves; in turn, we are set free from our fallen nature, being reborn into a new nature in Christ. Salvation is the restoration of humility. Jesus' humility becomes our salvation, and his salvation becomes our humility. Christians should bear witness to their salvation and restoration from the sin of pride. Regardless of the stage of our spiritual journey, pride should be our greatest adversary and humility should be our closest companion.

Pride can be overcome only through the presence of Christ. His humility reminds us that sin does not diminish our worth. Sometimes, when our souls are burdened with shame and the consequences of our transgressions, we might mistake it for humility. However, this is only discouragement or shame, rather than true humility. Like tall, rigid bamboo, pride merely sways without breaking.

True humility lies in discovering our insignificance and lowering ourselves before the magnificence of God's grace. Thus, humility requires not sin but grace. It is through realizing how insignificant we are in the presence of the One who bestows everything on us that we can experience true humility. We become humble as we humble ourselves before our God.

A tree laden with fruit bends its branches, and a river during a flood deepens its course. Similarly, only those who live in union with Christ's death can attain humility. We die to our sins, and through faith in the power of the gospel manifested on the cross of Christ, we reach true humility.

The people of this world will find it difficult to encounter Jesus if they cannot find humility among their leaders and within the church, the body of Christ. The diminishing presence of humility within the church signifies a departure from the presence of Jesus Christ. Above all, the humility of Christ must manifest in pastors. That is why I must confess that I myself have become the greatest obstacle in my pastoral ministry. These days, I yearn to reflect deeply on my ministry, examining whether I may have lost humility at some point along the way.

# 32

# ONLY SHEPHERDS
# ANSWERED THE CALL

THE INITIAL CHRISTMAS EVENT unfolded amid a world steeped in indifference. Indifference often stems from ignorance, and the world remains utterly unaware of the significance of the Messiah's birth. Yet the angels could not remain silent. They were the sole witnesses privy to the secrets of the spiritual world.

It was the angels who first announced the birth of the Messiah to the shepherds. According to the Gospel of Matthew, the three magi came to worship the infant Jesus after some time had passed, while he was residing in a house (see Matthew 2:11). In contrast, the shepherds arrived when Jesus was still lying in the manger.

Why is this detail important? To comprehend its significance, we must understand the social status of the shepherds at that time. They were individuals who dwelled on the outskirts of Bethlehem, residing in fields and sleeping alongside their sheep at night. They were inconspicuous and marginalized in society. The Gospel of Matthew highlights that it was these humble individuals who first received news of the Messiah's birth.

Information is power. Typically, when news breaks, it is first told to individuals of high rank and great influence. The level, amount, and nature of information and how it is disseminated typically varies depending on one's position and authority. The world's order revolves around access to information.

But what about the shepherds? In that society, shepherds dwelling outside the castle gate were not highly esteemed, and they had limited knowledge of what transpired within those walls. They lacked political opinions and social influence. And yet news of the Messiah's birth reached them first. The most crucial and urgent tidings were entrusted to the most alienated and lowly members of society. This was revolutionary.

Through this event God proclaims that no one is insignificant. God actively works through those who appear marginalized and lowly to deliver the message of the gospel. The power and blessings of the gospel manifest in the world not through the wealthy but through the poor. While the world may discriminate against certain individuals, God does not engage in such discrimination. On the contrary, God stands in solidarity with those who suffer, willingly embracing weakness alongside the weak.

Max Lucado, a renowned author and pastor, offered an intriguing perspective in a Christmas sermon. He mused that if the Pharisees had been the first to hear the news, they would have delved into biblical commentaries and organized seminars. If politicians had received the news, they would have wasted time scrutinizing eyewitness accounts. If entrepreneurs had been the initial recipients, they would have fixated on their calendars, trying to fit it into their schedules. The reason the shepherds, rather than great entrepreneurs or strategists, were the first to receive this remarkable news was that they believed and promptly acted on what they heard.

Now, did only the shepherds hear the angelic proclamation? Morton Kelsey, in his book *The Drama of Christmas*, suggests that others may have also received the news. The fact that God conveyed the news to the magi through a mysterious star implies that he could have communicated the Messiah's birth to everyone in various ways. Kelsey suggests that the news may have reached those comfortably sleeping in their Bethlehem homes through dreams. Angels may have appeared to merchants, innkeepers, and even the residents of King Herod's palace. However, all these people remained in bed, dismissing the strange dreams from the previous night as mere fancy. Only the shepherds wholeheartedly accepted the angels' words.

Immediately after receiving the angelic message, the shepherds did not convene seminars to debate its meaning. Instead of wasting time in futile arguments, they abandoned their flock and hurriedly went to worship Jesus.

God delivers his message to those who know how to respond to it. Therefore, what brings God the greatest joy is our swift response to his message and our willingness to be people of faith who promptly take action.

# 33

# THE TRUE LEADER STEPS
# UP IN THE STORM

꒰

GEORGE HERBERT (1592-1633) SAID, "He that will learn
to pray, let him go to sea." Does this imply that prayer can be
learned while basking in the serenity of a beautiful beach? Not
necessarily. It means that prayer can be learned amid the tempes-
tuous waves of a storm.

A storm cares not for one's social status, career, or wealth. In
the face of a storm, all hope seems lost without exception. We are
confronted with our own powerlessness and lack of foresight. It
is in these storms that God's sovereignty is revealed to humanity.

When we contemplate the storms of our lives, the figure of Job
often comes to mind. He engaged in discussions with his friends
and presented his pleas before God amid his weariness, posing
numerous questions. God did not engage in a calm discussion
with Job. Instead, he appeared within the storm and responded
to Job. It was in the midst of the storm that Job encountered God.

The storm serves as a means to redirect those who have strayed
from God's plan. Jonah, the embodiment of disobedience, exemplifies this truth. He encountered a storm while aboard a ship
bound for Tarshish, despite God's command to go to Nineveh.
God revealed himself as the storm, casting Jonah into the sea and
prompting his repentance. Jonah, too, saw God within the storm.

The storm serves as a pathway for the Lord to reach those plagued by fear. As Lake Galilee was whipped into a tempest, the once-calm waters surged to great heights before crashing down. It was amid this storm that the disciples beheld the Lord, who reassured them, saying, "It is I. Don't be afraid" (Matthew 14:27). After the storm subsided, the disciples worshiped Jesus. Never before had they worshiped with such unity of heart. There is no record of the disciples worshiping even when Jesus healed the sick or preached to the crowds. It was only when he walked amid the storm that they worshiped him because they were saved in a situation where all hope seemed lost.

Sometimes storms arise as a result of our own greed. God allows humanity to encounter great storms in order to quell our selfish desires for haste and profit. This was the case when the ship carrying Paul to Rome encountered a massive storm known as *Euraquilo*, or "northeastern wind."

In that storm, the Lord was with Paul. Paul assumed the role of a spiritual captain aboard a ship adrift in the tempest. The storm revealed his spiritual leadership. A storm does not create a leader, but it unveils the true leader.

Because Paul was deeply rooted in the presence of God, he remained steadfast amid the storm. Paul acted and carried himself according to his faith. Even when they had nothing to eat during the storm, he urged the crew and passengers to eat with ease, as if nothing were amiss (see Acts 27:33-37). Paul had faith in what God had bestowed on him, and his faith provided him with composure and gratitude, enabling him to eat.

People found solace in observing Paul's unwavering faith. Although the situation had not changed, they viewed it differently than before. Encouraged, they overcame their fear of perishing. It is not merely the words of a leader that people follow; they observe the leader's actions.

The world resembles a ship in distress, adrift without hope. In such times Christians are called to be spiritual captains who can instill faith and courage in the world. An angel of God told Paul, "God has graciously given you the lives of all who sail with you" (Act 27:24). God had entrusted the lives of all 276 aboard to his apostle.

The church must take the spiritual initiative to guide those who despair amid the storm. To do so, we must anchor ourselves deeply in the presence of God. The church must repent and turn away from the path of self-imposed disobedience. We must acknowledge God's sovereignty and willingly engage in his work without complaint or resentment, even in the face of suffering. We must rediscover the true essence of worship amid the storm. When these changes occur, God will employ the church as the spiritual captain of a ship navigating through the storm.

Like a ship navigating through a violent storm, the church may find itself engulfed by tumultuous circumstances. Instead of indulging in a blame game, it is crucial to acknowledge that the root cause of this turmoil lies in the church's own disobedience. Our nation is weathering this tempest because church leaders have fallen short in purging themselves of the destructive force of greed.

Ralph Waldo Emerson (1803–1882) remarked, "The wise man in the storm prays to God not for safety from danger but for deliverance from fear." The church must learn the true essence of prayer amid the storm. We must turn away from disobedience and forge ahead in the direction intended by God. Our future remains uncertain unless the church assumes the role of a spiritual captain before the storm intensifies and engulfs everything. Only those who act in accordance with the will of God, the master of the storm, remain unshaken by its fury.

# 34

# EMBRACING CONFLICT

მ

IN ANY COMMUNITY, WHEN CONFLICT ARISES, two unde-
sirable results often emerge. The first is the perspective that mag-
nifies the conflict even more than its actual seriousness. Instead
of objectively examining the causes of the conflict, this position
subjectively involves one's distorted emotions, exacerbating
the situation.

The second perspective is a refusal to acknowledge the existence of conflict, choosing to avoid or deny it. This stance avoids
precise identification of the conflict's roots and hastily covers it
up, mistakenly believing that the conflict is resolved.

Renowned American social activist Parker Palmer, in his book
*Healing the Heart of Democracy*, emphasized that creatively embracing tension and conflict and transforming them into new
energy is the true strength of democracy. He posited that in a
democratic system, tension and conflict are not problems themselves but rather the starting points for a healthy democracy.

Approaching tension and conflict subjectively by either magnifying or avoiding them is detrimental to democracy. Thus,
Palmer stressed the significance of addressing the issues of the
heart within democracy. Healing the heart through the creative
embrace of tension and conflict should be primarily experienced
in faith-based communities.

So, how can we creatively embrace tension and transform it into new energy? How can we ensure that conflicts lead to maturity in the community rather than strife and division?

The solution lies in maintaining relationships where opposing views are allowed and respected. A community that does not allow for differences or opposing viewpoints cannot mature. When a community deteriorates due to tension and conflict, it often demands unquestioning agreement with the leader's perspectives and does not allow any dissent. It treats those with different thoughts as enemies and severs relationships.

People who carry the wounds of rejection are often quick to respond with excessive anger and aggression toward opposing views due to their fear of rejection. Alternatively, they may refuse to engage in any form of relationship and resist joining the community.

In most cases, individuals outwardly agree even when they inwardly disagree with those they are close to because they fear the consequences of severing relationships. Instead of courageously speaking the truth with love, they succumb to the fear of disrupting the relationship.

Those who openly express their disagreements contribute to the maturation of the community more than those who keep their dissent and bitterness inside. The way in which they receive opposing views plays a crucial role in either bringing maturity or crisis to the community. It ultimately comes down to matters of the heart. By honestly stating "no," the people within a community who creatively embrace tension may end up loving the community more.

A community that maintains relationships allowing for the free expression of opposing views, even among those close to each other, can withstand tensions and conflicts without damage. If individuals can freely express "no" while having an open heart, they may eventually be willing to say "yes" to the right opinions, even if they initially disagree.

In unhealthy political communities, there is a culture of uncritical agreement with those close in opinion and uncritical opposition to those in opposition. It's a typical characteristic of communities on the brink of collapse. However, the mere recognition and respect of the freedom to disagree does not automatically lead to community maturity. Humility is needed on the part of those opposing as well. After all, tension and conflict can be healed only with a humble heart. Those opposed also need to have a heart that creatively embraces tension.

A common trap for those who find reasons to oppose is the tendency to justify their opposition. It's a destructive pride. They cannot see the poison hidden in their opposition. To truly progress as a community, those who oppose must have the humility to face their own motivations. Conflict and tension are ultimately resolved through the humility of both sides. Those opposing should also have a heart that embraces tension creatively.

People who discover reasons to oppose often fall into the trap of justifying their opposition. It's a destructive form of arrogance. To advance as a community, those who oppose must humbly confront their motivations. Conflict and tension are ultimately resolved through the humility of both parties. Those who oppose should also have a heart that creatively embraces tension.

Today's society—in politics, education, culture, religion, and all fields, really—demonstrates the necessity of cultivating a heart that can creatively embrace tension as advocated by Palmer. Before addressing the divisive issues, we must look beneath the surface to understand each other's hearts and examine our own. To avoid becoming a society engulfed in inevitable tension and conflict, we need the courage to express dissent.

# 35

# LOOK TO THE SELF, THEN
# THE SITUATION

LEADERS OFTEN FIND THEMSELVES facing crises and navigating through numerous dilemmas that shape the course of history. To address these dilemmas, they must possess discretion—an ability to grasp the essence of the problem and find solutions. It is akin to untangling a knotted thread, charting a course without a map, or devising an unprecedented mathematical formula to solve an unsolvable problem.

But how can leaders cultivate discretion? Many initially rely on situational analysis. They listen to others, pay attention to their perspectives, and assess the situation. While these steps are necessary, decisive discretion in solving dilemmas cannot be solely derived from examining the situation or public opinion.

Discretion springs forth from the leader's inner analysis. It particularly stems from a deep introspection of one's emotions. First and foremost, leaders must examine whether their dilemma is rooted in their own emotional responses. Have their words and decisions concerning the situation been influenced by negative emotions such as hatred or fear? If not, leaders must also evaluate their emotional disposition toward the dilemma itself. Are they gripped by fear, or are they displaying genuine courage that surpasses their fears?

Blaise Pascal (1623–1662), a French philosopher, aptly wrote in *Pensées*, "All of our reasoning ends in surrender to feeling." Injured feelings possess a fearsome power to undermine rational judgment. If leaders have faced dilemmas and experienced the pain of making incorrect decisions driven by speculative feelings, Pascal's words serve as a piercing admonition. Despite having reasoned speculations, one often loses rationality because of the dominance of overwhelming emotions.

Ignatius of Loyola (1491–1556), a Spanish reformer and the founder of the Jesuits, emphasized that in situations requiring discretion, the primary focus should be on discerning one's feelings rather than the external circumstances. Discerning one's inner feelings through rational judgment is a crucial prerequisite for cultivating discretion.

We can learn wisdom in obtaining exceptional discretion from Solomon's example. When God appeared to Solomon after he became the king of Israel, God did not say, "Now that you are king, I will grant you the wisdom of discretion that you need the most." Instead, God asked Solomon, "Ask for whatever you want me to give you" (see 1 Kings 3:5). This offer was significant since it shows us that knowing what one truly needs is of utmost importance for a leader.

If God were to ask us, "What do you want me to give you?" would we be prepared with our answer? Those who fail to realize what they truly need in their lives will not ask for it, regardless of the abundant grace God bestows on them. Solomon asked for the wisdom of discretion—the very thing he knew he needed most as a king to navigate the many dilemmas he would face. His earnest request exemplifies the attitude of mind we should adopt toward discretion: humility.

Solomon humbly acknowledged that his ascent to kingship was a result of God's great grace on his father, David, in the past. He openly admitted that as a king he lacked a discerning heart (see 1 Kings 3:6-9). He approached God with humility.

Humility entails honestly examining ourselves in light of the truth. If leaders harbor only sentimental and idealistic thoughts about themselves, they will fail to discern situations accurately. We must recognize that as human beings we are fragile and in need of God's assistance. We must admit that our thoughts are not infallible, regardless of how right they may seem. That is humility.

At times we must also acknowledge that the solution may come from those who stand against us. If an answer presents itself that ensures the survival and well-being of all, even if it doesn't originate from our own thoughts or opinions, we must courageously embrace it. Though the link between humility and discretion may appear abstract, it embodies the most practical truth. Humility purifies our emotions and guides us toward rational judgment.

I earnestly pray that leaders possess the wisdom to solve the dilemmas facing our nation and its people in this age of crisis.

# 36

# REAL CHANGE

VAGUE HOPES OR POSITIVE THINKING cannot bring about true change in history. What truly alters the course of history is radical and fundamental repentance. The English word *radical* finds its roots in the Latin word *radix*, which means "root." Hence, radical repentance signifies a deep return to one's roots, identifying and uprooting the destructive roots. In considering Jesus' warning to the church of Laodicea, we can discern valuable lessons on how to turn back to Christ.

> I know your deeds, that you are neither cold nor hot. I wish you were either one or the other! So, because you are lukewarm—neither hot nor cold—I am about to spit you out of my mouth. (Revelation 3:15-16)

First and foremost, we must turn away from a faith mixed with idols and return to sincere and genuine worship. The phrase "to be either cold or hot" in reference to the church of Laodicea does not simply mean "to believe or not to believe." It signifies that being completely cold or hot is preferable to being lukewarm. The lukewarm faith of the Laodicean church does not denote a moderately immature faith but rather an insincere faith tainted by idol worship. True faith demands wholehearted commitment and honesty. If our faith is genuine, we must wholeheartedly embrace and embody it. If it is false, we must wholeheartedly reject and oppose it. What is perplexing is the lukewarm attitude and dubious indifference that arise when idol worship infiltrates our faith.

When we serve a mixture of God and idols, our faith becomes as tainted as the lukewarm water in Laodicea. Falsehood always attempts to camouflage itself as truth, and idolatry perpetually lurks behind genuine faith. Whenever genuine faith appears to wane, idolatry rears its ugly head. We must transform our faith mixed with idols into a faith that is true and pure.

Furthermore, let us turn away from a life focused on the pursuit of material abundance and instead seek spiritual abundance. The pursuit of material wealth should not be confused with the pursuit of spiritual richness. Materialistic pursuits can easily distract us from the true abundance found in our relationship with God. Our lives should not be driven solely by the accumulation of possessions and wealth. Instead, we should prioritize spiritual growth, seeking the fullness and richness of a life centered on Christ.

To experience true transformation and restoration, the church must respond to God's call to repentance. We must forsake lukewarm and insincere faith, turning instead to a genuine and committed faith. Additionally, we should redirect our focus from material abundance to spiritual richness. May the church embrace radical repentance and witness the power of God's transformative work in our midst.

> You say, "I am rich; I have acquired wealth and do not need a thing." But you do not realize that you are wretched, pitiful, poor, blind and naked. I counsel you to buy from me gold refined in the fire, so you can become rich; and white clothes to wear, so you can cover your shameful nakedness; and salve to put on your eyes, so you can see. (Revelation 3:17-18)

The people of Laodicea were ensnared by self-satisfaction, believing that their accumulation of wealth would secure their well-being. Even among the Christians, this worldly mindset had taken hold, breeding a spirit of arrogance that permeated the church.

Yet these notions are nothing but foolish illusions. Consider our society today. Isn't it consumed with the pursuit of material prosperity, neglecting the state of the soul and elevating the economy as the supreme concern? If this continues, our souls will grow increasingly corrupt, even if the economy appears to flourish. In such a scenario, the very economy we idolize will eventually crumble.

Economic means and wealth are gracious blessings from God when we prioritize the well-being of our souls, morality, and spirituality. Regardless of the economic challenges we may face, we must resolve to live with honesty and integrity. We must embrace the belief that true happiness lies in honesty and that a life lived in righteousness is one of genuine abundance.

Furthermore, we must turn away from a life where Jesus is kept at a distance, treated as a mere visitor, and instead embrace a life of obedience where we invite the Lord to dwell within us.

Those whom I love I rebuke and discipline. So be earnest and repent. Here I am! I stand at the door and knock. If anyone hears my voice and opens the door, I will come in and eat with that person, and they with me. (Revelation 3:19-20)

What does true repentance entail? It involves acknowledging and surrendering to the Lord's sovereignty. Revelation 3:20 calls us to repent, often being used as an invitation to unbelievers or new believers to open their hearts and accept Jesus as Lord. However, its deeper significance lies in restoring a genuine relationship with the Lord for those who have shut Jesus out. The verse urges us to repent, turn around, and recognize the Lord as the true master of our lives.

Many of us proclaim Jesus as Lord during worship in the church, but when we return to our daily lives, we often set him aside. This applies not only to congregants but even to pastors. Jesus' will, character, and sovereignty do not manifest in their lives.

We must acknowledge Jesus as Lord not just within the confines of the chapel but also in the world. When this occurs, our attitude toward the world changes. Jesus embraced the world, and if we confess him as Lord, we cannot turn away from souls thirsting for the gospel amid the darkness of the world. We cannot ignore our alienated neighbors.

The church must relinquish its self-centered attitude and ask the question, "What would Jesus do in this situation?" All questions will find their answers. When the church embraces Jesus' sovereignty and turns around, the world will change.

# 37

# KNOW THYSELF

ALTHOUGH GREEK PHILOSOPHERS WROTE "know thyself" on the entrance of the Delphic temple, humans can never truly know themselves. The Reformer John Calvin began the first book of his *Institutes of the Christian Religion* with the idea that the knowledge of God and the knowledge of oneself are interconnected. He wrote, "True and sound wisdom consists entirely of two parts: the knowledge of God and of ourselves." People, he explained, must first meditate on the face of God and then descend to examine themselves carefully; otherwise they will not reach true self-knowledge. In other words, one can only attain true knowledge of oneself when encountering the Creator God. To know God one must know oneself, and one who has not reached true self-discovery has either not met God at all or is not meeting him in the proper way.

Jesus taught about the close connection between the knowledge of oneself and the knowledge of God through the parable of the prayers of two people (see Luke 18:10-14). Prayer is a window into the soul that shows us how we perceive God and how we understand ourselves.

In the parable, there are two characters: one is a Pharisee and the other is a tax collector. The Pharisee was a representative saint of the time, and the tax collector was a representative sinner.

The two have similarities. They both confess something about themselves while praying. How they perceive and discover themselves, however, is very dissimilar. In addition, Jesus' evaluation overturns our expectations. Jesus did not accept the prayer of the Pharisee but recognized the prayer of the tax collector as righteous. The reason why is that the Pharisee exalted himself while the tax collector humbled himself.

The Pharisee prayed about himself while standing. Although he called on God, he was, in essence, giving a monologue directed toward himself. His prayer had no windows, so he could not look at God. He was simply trapped in a room with himself, talking to himself. His prayer had gratitude, but not for what God had done. It was gratitude only for what he himself had done. This is self-satisfaction. In his prayer, he did not repent and instead compared himself to others, believing himself to be holy. This is self-righteousness. In his prayer, there was no supplication to God. This is self-dependence. In his prayer, there was pride and hypocrisy because he believed that he did more than his duty to faith. This is self-glorification.

On the other hand, the tax collector recognized himself as deserving punishment before God. Augustine said, "Nothing is nearer to your ears than a confessing heart and a life grounded in faith." He confessed that he was a sinner. He desperately sought God's grace. The most important reason the tax collector's prayer was recognized by Jesus was that he evaluated himself only by looking up at God. The standard of evaluation for ourselves should be only God. When God and his Word are the only criteria for evaluating ourselves, we can achieve true self-discovery.

But we can become like Pharisees even when we pray like a tax collector, confessing ourselves as sinners and seeking God's grace. That is a frightening reality. We must repent only before God, not comparing ourselves to any other person. There must be only a deep confession of our need for God's grace. Without true self-discovery, there can be no true salvation experience. If you have experienced God's salvation, you must experience true self-discovery. Prayer must become an important path for self-discovery before God.

# 38

# FAITH OR STUBBORNNESS?

THE KOREAN LANGUAGE HAS A WORD for an older person who is condescending, who always looks on younger generations with disdain, and who is the human manifestation of the "been there; done that" mentality—*kkon-dae*. The *kkon-dae* can be found anywhere—not just in Korea, but in any culture, and in any society.

As people age, some tend to expand their social circle while others shrink it. There is rarely an in-between. With increasing life experience, those who possess a broad understanding of themselves, others, and the world find a sense of peace. However, even if two individuals share similar experiences, one individual may be more self-centered, caring solely for their own interests, and this can lead to becoming a *kkon-dae*. Age and experience do not automatically make someone a mature adult.

We see this in our churches. Those who take pride in their years of faith often exhibit self-righteousness, narrow-mindedness, and self-satisfaction. Externally, they may appear to express spiritual confidence, but in reality they are just stubborn. They mistake their stubbornness for faith, failing to recognize their "wisdom" as the sin of pride.

True faith entails relying on something other than oneself. For the Christian, this is Jesus. Meanwhile, stubbornness involves placing faith in one's own self. True faith involves entrusting one's thoughts and will to Jesus, whereas stubbornness manipulates Jesus to protect one's thoughts and will. Unfortunately, many actions carried out in the name of Jesus are used to justify the shallow stubbornness of individuals. As faith grows stronger, one increasingly denies oneself, but as stubbornness intensifies, one fortifies oneself.

As one matures, it can be challenging to discern between faith and stubbornness. Outwardly, the manifestations of either may appear similar. Both faith and stubbornness can be characterized by perseverance and a refusal to give up in the face of dissension and difficulties. However, as time progresses, they bear distinctive fruit. Faith ultimately brings about desirable changes and peace, whereas stubbornness leads to appropriation, strife, and division. Faith guides others toward truth, while stubbornness keeps others away from it.

There is emerging evidence that true faith is lacking in this age. The church seems to have become the *kkon-dae* of our era, a self-centered old man who spurns the young and condescends to everyone who may hold a different opinion. This is the consequence of mistakenly believing and reinforcing the stubborn adherence to a familiar church culture simply because it is familiar. We confuse stubbornness with faith.

Nothing can replace the act of relinquishing our stubbornness and embracing true faith. This is a personal choice for every Christian. The question we must ask ourselves each day is whether the guiding principle of our lives is faith or stubbornness. It is a question of faith that we cannot disregard, one we must continually answer.

# 39

# TIME FOR JOB'S REPENTANCE

GOD PUTS THE RIGHTEOUS JOB to the test to verify whether he fears God because of the blessings he has received or not. Satan is given permission by God to attack Job with any calamity, except for his life. Job's suffering takes place in three stages.

The first stage of suffering is when all Job's possessions suddenly disappear in a single day. Everything he has enjoyed abundantly vanishes unexpectedly in a moment during a family feast. However, Job does not sin or blame God. Instead, he submits to God's goodness and praises him.

The second stage of suffering is when a severe disease befalls Job himself. Malignant sores spring up all over his body. Will he react the same way when suffering an unbearable disease as he did when he lost all his children and possessions? In the midst of this second trial, Job does not abandon his faith in God's goodness.

The third stage of suffering entails enduring continuous pressure for an extended period. Job has to endure the "comforting words" of his friends. Each time his three friends add a word of comfort, Job's pain increases. If his friends had not come and offered their comfort, he might have endured the pain in silence. Hearing their words, he faces an even tougher test of faith. Job has to go through a long night of spiritual darkness.

Momentary pain and suffering may be bearable, but enduring constant pain is difficult. After listening to his friends for seven days, Job finally opens his mouth. When he does so, his sighs and lamentations burst forth, not out of blame toward God, but with doubts about God's righteousness for allowing such immense suffering to come on him, one who had lived righteously and piously. However, in the presence of God's arrival amid the storm, Job repents.

Through suffering, Job discovered the pride that lay deep inside his soul. He could assert that he had no sinful or impure life fitting to be called a sinner, yet unbeknown to him, a hidden sin lurked in his heart. That sin was self-righteousness.

God reveals our hidden self-righteousness through deep darkness and leads us to repentance. Even righteous people like Job need to repent—how much more, then, do we need to repent? Still, God gradually reveals our sins. If he revealed them all at once, we might give up on life out of despair.

True repentance is acknowledging that no matter how severe our sufferings, God is good and righteous. Suffering is not a process of breaking us down but of revealing God's work through darkness. It is a process of uncovering the pride and sin hidden within us and purifying us even more.

God exposes the terrifying self-righteousness hidden within us and leads us to repentance. This is why Job's repentance is necessary for us.

# 40

# GOD LOVES CITIES OF SINNERS

IN MODERN SOCIETY, the phenomenon of urban concentration seems like an unsolvable problem. Cities have become the central backbone of almost every field—including political, economic, educational, social, and cultural spheres. The horrifying corruption taking place in the shadows of large cities is more than enough to support a negative view of urban life.

Jacques Ellul, in his book *The Meaning of the City*, describes cities as a result of relying on one's own strength and pursuing security apart from God. He cites Cain as an example, who built the first city after killing Abel to seek peace and rest for himself, and the builders of the Tower of Babel, who dreamed of a world without God and built a gigantic city. Ellul argues that God is angry at the city itself and that cities inherently become the epitome of social sin. He claims that cities are cursed not because of the particular sins of the people who inhabit them but because they participate in the evil forces that are socially defined by the cities.

Ellul's argument is based on the idea that everything in the world centered on cities is evil. He categorizes everything in the city as evil and unrelated to the Word of God. Although Ellul's reflection on the evil of cities has provided great introspection for humanity rushing toward urban centers, his views remain ignorant of the biblical and missiological significance of cities.

Throughout church history, there were serious consequences when theological reflections on cities were neglected and the missiological significance of cities was ignored. When the church defined cities solely as Sodom filled with sin and fled from and abandoned them, it lost its missionary influence and became trapped in the world. Many churches are built in the hearts of European cities, but they have now become mission fields themselves.

God's cultural mandate to Adam does not limit humanity to the garden (see Genesis 1:28). In fact, it could even be said that God intended humanity to build cities. People were commanded to be stewards of the earth, to manage and govern creation and its resources. If cities had not been influenced by sin, they could have been extraordinary hubs of culture and accomplishment beyond our imagination.

Would God then give up on a city with a corrupted culture? No. He is the One who does not give up on even fallen humans. There is no chance he would give up on cities where such people gather. Rather, he looks at cities with a missiological perspective. The more sinners there are, the more grace can abound, as he said. That's why the apostle Paul traveled through the cities of Asia and Europe preaching, and the gospel spread from city to city as it reached them.

Through cities, God prepares a holy city for us at the end. The holy city, called the new Jerusalem, descends from heaven from God, an untainted and pure place uncontaminated by sin. Life in this city is peaceful and harmonious. Death and sorrow disappear, and there is no more pain. Everything that once tarnished the former city vanishes forever. Most importantly, God will dwell in complete communion with the people. This holy city is where the Lamb, Christ, who sacrificed himself for sinners' redemption, is present, and he will receive praise from all the city's inhabitants.

The Bible teaches that the coming future world will be an urban world. The drama of redemption starts in the Garden of Eden and ends in the city of the new Jerusalem. Heaven's citizens will ultimately be city dwellers. Today's cities are full of sin, falsehood, corruption, immorality, malice, idolatry, and greed. The streets and markets overflow with sin. Yet God still loves cities. If the misunderstanding that God hates cities is not discarded, we commit the sin of rejecting God's grace. The God who loves the world loves cities where fallen sinners gather. That's why he bestows common grace on the city and even allows it to prosper.

The future is like a strange place that we have never been to before. When we travel to unfamiliar places, we rely on maps. No matter how complicated the roads are, we can travel if we have a map. However, imagine someone trying to travel around present-day Seoul using a map from a hundred years ago. It would be impossible for him to find his way. Likewise, to travel into the approaching future, we need a new map that is suitable for the future. The question is, who will create this map? Some people wait until someone else makes a map. Yet pioneers create their own maps before anyone else steps up.

We are in a situation similar to the Israelites on the banks of the Jordan River. After forty years of wilderness life, the Israelites embarked on a journey back to Canaan. A new way of life was needed for this new journey. The old way of life in the wilderness was not sufficient for the uncharted path to Canaan. The unbelievers would say, "Let's return to a familiar and seemingly safe place." However, true faith calls for advancing into the place where God works while taking risks to create a new map.

None of the Israelites, except for Joshua and Caleb, had ever crossed the Red Sea. They were a new generation born in the wilderness. Although they might have heard stories about the miracles at the Red Sea from their parents when the Israelites left Egypt, they only stood and watched the flooded Jordan River. The Jordan River was the gateway to enter into the Promised Land of life as granted by God. It was an obstacle that could not be crossed by human power alone.

At this point Joshua gave a command to the people: "'Consecrate yourselves, for tomorrow the LORD will do amazing things among you.' Joshua said to the priests, 'Take up the ark of the covenant and pass on ahead of the people.' So they took it up and went ahead of them" (Joshua 3:5-6). Joshua informed the people that God would do amazing things the next day. He had expectations and faith in the God who will be operating tomorrow.

The word emphasized by the commanders and Joshua is *ahead*. The ark of the covenant going ahead signifies the presence of God leading them. God is not only a companion but also someone who moves ahead of his people. God does not just command his people to go on an uncharted path; he leads them by going ahead personally. A person who believes in such a God never fears or despairs about the future. A person who knows God's love can stand firm against any situation in this world.

God only moves one step ahead so that we can follow. If God moved so far ahead that we could not even see him, we would not be able to follow him. So God moves just ahead of us.

God, who goes ahead, leads us with methods we cannot fully understand for purposes that are difficult to fathom. God's purpose was to establish Joshua's leadership through the process of crossing the Jordan River. It was not just to address the immediate problem but to prepare for the future conquest of Canaan.

The God who led Israel into the Promised Land also sends us into situations that we cannot understand. As we walk through life, we encounter experiences that confuse us, hurt us, or even break us. We cannot fully grasp God's purpose. However, God does not permit anything without reason. Everything that happens to us is part of the process in which God, who goes ahead, fulfills his purpose. Even if we cannot understand it, we must believe in God's actions. God, who goes ahead, performs amazing things on the path we have never been on before.

Some people say that there are no amazing things that God does in their lives. This is because they always rely on their own familiar steps. But our souls awaken when God leads us on an unfamiliar path. At that time we become tense and seek God's guidance. We wait for and follow the words that God gives us.

When we encounter an unknown path in front of us, it means that God has given us a new command. God, who goes ahead, provides the necessary commands promptly at each stage. The opaque future ahead is an opportunity for us to hear God's extraordinary and new commands.

At times, cities can be a testament to God's general grace in preserving and restraining sin. God protects cities with the purpose of preserving humanity by controlling the tendencies of those who intend to destroy themselves. Although cities can spread sin, God works in the midst of them to prevent the spread of evil, protect his creations, and exercise his sovereignty. God works to restrain the sinful nature of people who try to turn cities into Babylon, and he works to transform them into spiritual Jerusalem instead. Cities are sites of enormous spiritual warfare, battlegrounds as various forces vie for sovereignty.

It is the responsibility of Christians to fight for the manifestation of special grace within cities if they view them as a testimony to God's general grace. Christians must not abandon the cities. They should focus on the mission of revealing the history of the gospel in cities. As Christ called us to be the salt and light of the world, we must become the salt and light of the city. The ancient city of Nineveh was a massive city filled with sin, and God sent Jonah there as a missionary.

God loves cities in this age and loves the many sinners who have gathered within them. He redeems them through the cross, bestows greater grace on them, and leads them to the city he has prepared for them.

PART FIVE

# LIVE OUT

# YOUR GOOD

# LIFE

# 41

# THE CHRISTIAN LIFE IS
# A SYNTROPY DRAMA

꒰

ON JULY 2, 2019, A MEMORIAL SERVICE took place at the main hall of Onnuri Church for the late Elder Young-gil Kim. One of the first elders of the church and the inaugural president of Handong Global University, a Christian university in Korea, Elder Kim was bid farewell with tears streaming down the faces of countless congregants and university alumni.

Elder Kim exemplified a life of sacrifice and service. He never sought self-glorification, emphasized his own righteousness, paraded his expertise, or imposed his authority anywhere, including with his family, church, or school. His influence and reputation stemmed from his humility—a spirituality that mirrored Jesus not only in his words but also in his sacrificial dedication. It is said that even in his final moments Elder Kim earnestly requested his family to praise only God and not himself.

The late Reverend Yong-jo Ha (1946–2011), the founder of Onnuri Church, declared, "Those who have been trained in this church for seven years should go out and change the world." Elder Kim was the first to heed this message from Reverend Ha. He wholeheartedly devoted himself to establishing Handong Global University in the unassuming town of Pohang, relinquishing his secure position as a professor at the Korea Advanced Institute of Science and Technology (KAIST).

Undoubtedly, he encountered hardships including false accusations and imprisonment, but he believed in the vision bestowed on him. He was a servant of God and so walked the path with unwavering commitment, disregarding personal gain or loss. Even as his health declined, he poured his heart and passion into founding the Ki-moon Ban Institute of Global Education through the United Nations Academic Impact initiative. On his deathbed, he burned with a final desire to share the experiences he had at Handong Global University with the world. His life can rightly be called a great drama—a divine drama.

All our lives are dramas orchestrated and directed by God. Yet people are often reluctant to accept God as the ultimate authority who oversees, governs, and provides for us—the author of our story. We desire to control the outcomes of our lives according to our own preferences. However, our lives rarely unfold precisely as we plan because there is a greater Planner at work. God presides over our lives, governs us, and will ultimately judge us.

Elder Kim's life became a captivating drama that touched the hearts of many because he lived in complete obedience to God the Creator. In every chapter of his obedient life, God's work became evident.

In God's great narrative, crises always arise, and sometimes unbearable pain accompanies them. However, when we obey the Word, the crises and hardships that come are evidence that God is with us. God turns every crisis into a beautiful moment of growth. A bland drama will fail to leave an impression. A memorable story always has tension, extremes, and crises that seem unbearable. But in the best dramas, and even in God's dramas, there is always a twist.

In the life of Elder Kim, too, there was a divine twist. It is well reflected in his work *Syntropy Drama*, which he wrote during the final years of his life. Entropy, a concept that many people know, describes a state of increasing disorder, like a human gradually debilitating toward "rock bottom." Many might claim that all human life will succumb to entropy but Elder Kim believed otherwise. He claimed that syntropy, the opposite of entropy, is what characterizes life and that humanity is not destined for disorder or destruction. Absence is transformed into creation, and death is transformed into life. When an old fruit falls to the ground and rots, a new one sprouts. Death is not the end. Even in the midst of this world, where everything is decaying and heading toward destruction, God shows us the law of spiritual syntropy, through which destruction is transformed into life.

His great drama is not over. God has already started the work of syntropy within us and within the world. The great climax of the story already occurred through the resurrection of Jesus Christ. His resurrection life has been granted to all of us and we, the protagonists of this drama, will see our happy ending—our eternal afterlife.

However, the term *afterlife* is a bit of a misnomer. It is more accurate to call our earthly life a *pre-life* period. The Word of God is the foundation of the syntropy narrative. We all had lives on this earth governed by the law of entropy, but now, in Christ, we become the protagonists of God's kingdom and his syntropy drama. Elder Kim proved that by simply and obediently following God's Word the syntropy drama will continue.

Elder Kim firmly believed in the syntropy drama. He believed that God, the Creator, governs through his Word. Just a few days before his passing, he confessed, "Even if I die, I will live. Death is a delight."

# 42

# YOUR MISSION IS TO GO
# BEYOND YOUR BACKYARD

IN MARCH 1987, THE LOCAL GOVERNMENT OF ISLIP, a city in New York, spent six months searching for a place to dispose of their waste, exploring six neighboring states and three countries, but failed to find a location anywhere. The term *NIMBY* (Not In My Backyard) was coined at that time, becoming the slogan of the residents who were deeply opposed to the dumping of their own waste so close to their homes.

Certainly, there are times when the NIMBY sentiment can be justified—for instance, objecting to the construction of amusement parks or gambling facilities that harm children. However, it is not desirable to object to public facilities merely because of residents' reluctance or the potential decrease in housing prices.

In Korea, the establishment of welfare facilities catering to individuals with developmental disabilities serves as a prominent case in point. Several years ago, a deeply impactful incident took place when parents of students with developmental disabilities knelt and fervently pleaded before residents who opposed the construction of a disability center. The powerful imagery from that article continues to resonate within me. It is disheartening to observe how political leaders, acutely aware of the residents' opposition, dare not envision the establishment of such facilities that inevitably become targets of the NIMBY phenomenon. Their success in deftly resolving such contentious issues is often deemed an indicator of their leadership abilities.

Recently, in some areas of Seoul, there have been cases of opposition to the installation of public childcare centers in apartment complexes or park areas. The biggest challenge in the era of low birthrates for Koreans is ensuring a safe place for children, yet the construction of childcare centers is often opposed on account of noise complaints. This goes against the fundamental tenets of responsible urban development, which is based on the needs of the city and its residents. Opposing even facilities where children receive education is taking the NIMBY attitude to an unhealthy extreme.

The mission and Christian values of the church should convict us to go beyond NIMBY. To achieve this, the church must first address any NIMBY attitudes within its own congregation. Even community decisions within the church can sometimes be influenced by localist self-centeredness.

The Sanmaru Church of South Korea faced an important decision due to frequent visits by homeless individuals. Some existing congregants threatened to leave the church if it continued to welcome the homeless. However, Pastor Joo-yon Lee continued welcoming the homeless as equal members of his congregation, which led to some other members leaving. Through this choice, the church overcame the NIMBY sentiment that had emerged within its own community. The growth of the church may have temporarily stalled by this incident, but God's kingdom flourished.

Furthermore, Sanmaru Church has made continuous efforts to establish bathhouses and shower facilities for the homeless. When constructing these facilities in the future, they may have to fight against even greater NIMBY opposition. However, this fight is extremely valuable and must be won. If the church gives up on this fight, it will remain just a church for the church's sake, rather than becoming a shining beacon in society. For the church to exist as the salt and light of the world, it must dissolve like salt in food, not through selfish individualism but through sacrifice and empathy.

In my perspective, it is imperative for the church to place a higher priority on marginalized groups compared to public institutions or other charitable organizations. South Korea is a nation that harbors over two million immigrants, people with disabilities, and homeless individuals, all of whom deserve to be embraced as a primary focus of our care and support.

When NIMBY pushes people to oppose constructing community centers or welfare facilities for these populations, the church should step forward and embrace them with love. Remember the words "Truly I tell you, whatever you did for one of the least of these brothers and sisters of mine, you did for me" (Matthew 25:40). When the church loves the immigrants, the disabled, and the homeless in each community, the kingdom of God grows. As a result, society will follow the example of the church, and the world will thrive.

# 43

# UNLOCK THE FUTURE WITH FAITH

❦

WHENEVER A NEW YEAR ARRIVES, I often observe two kinds
of people: those who eagerly anticipate it with hope and those
who approach it with anxiety.

Faith creates anticipation, while doubt fosters anxiety. A consistent strategy of the enemy is to make us worry, fret, and be
disappointed about the difficulties that lie ahead. The reason we
fret about the future is that we don't know what's going to happen.
If we knew everything that would occur in the future, would our
worries disappear? No, they would grow even more. Saint Augustine put it this way, "God does not tell us in advance about
future events because if we knew our successes, we would become
lazy, and conversely, if we knew our failures, we would become
disappointed and despondent."

The biblical history of Israel is marked by numerous instances
of unnecessary actions driven by worries about the future. A prime
example is the spying of Canaan. When you read Numbers 13,
you see that God instructed them to spy out the land of Canaan.
However, if you go further and read Deuteronomy 1, you'll find that
the idea of spying on Canaan was not originally God's. God had
initially told them to enter the Promised Land with faith, but due
to the people's fear and unbelief, they approached Moses, arguing
that they should scout the land first (see Deuteronomy 1:21-22).

Did this alleviate their fears and result in wisdom? No. The ten spies returned, causing even greater fear and dread among the people. Ultimately, this fear led to the people not entering the Promised Land, causing them to remain in the wilderness. Worries and anxieties generate unnecessary ideas.

God reveals to us only what we need to know about the future. He guides our lives like a sailing ship. At times, when the wind blows, the ship needs to pull back and endure storms. Without the wind, you won't move forward. The sailing ship has a cabin, but it doesn't always follow a clearly defined path. We often desire God to guide us like a train station, showing us every upcoming stop. Yet, God does not reveal all the stations at once; he shows us the next one if needed.

We demand a blueprint of life from God, but instead, he gives us a compass. A compass is useful when you're moving forward. If we trust the direction God is currently showing us and take one step at a time in faith, he continues to reveal new paths.

Our gracious God gives each of us the same future: tomorrow. He provides a new day for both successful and failed individuals. He doesn't give twice as many tomorrows to those who've succeeded in the past and half as many to those who've failed. The gracious God gives us a new day one by one. If you've failed today, he grants you a fresh start tomorrow.

There's a story of a pastor who visited a member of his church just before the member passed away. The pastor was surprised to hear the member say, "The doctor told me I have only two days left to live. Those are the most welcome words I've ever heard." When the pastor inquired further, the member explained, "I've always lived each day as if I only had one more day to live. But now, I've been told I have two days left; what joy!"

There was a time in Israel's history when the future seemed unclear, during the era when the prophet Isaiah was active. Politics, society, and morality were in decline, and the only thing remaining was God's judgment. Ironically, that's when God delivered some of the most hopeful messages. In Isaiah 40:1, God begins by saying, "Comfort, comfort my people." He continues to offer messages of hope throughout the sixty-six chapters.

During this time, Israel faced a future of being driven out into the wilderness, becoming servants to foreign powers, and countless deaths. Yet, God provided words of hope amid these circumstances. "Forget the former things; do not dwell on the past" (Isaiah 43:18), he said. In order to embrace a new tomorrow, you shouldn't be tied to the past. If you're attached to past successes, you might become arrogant; if you're attached to past failures, you might become discouraged, losing hope for the future. The past remains in our memories, and habits are memories of the past. Without renewing your memories, life won't change.

However, God also mentions that some things are worth remembering. In Isaiah 46:9, he says, "Remember the former things, those of long ago; I am God, and there is no other; I am God, and there is none like me." We should remember that there is no other God but him. We mustn't forget that we are his people. Remember that only God provides salvation and help in our lives. You must remember these things.

Youth is a time to dream about the future more than reminiscing about the past. Yet, the Bible doesn't tell young people to "dream about the future." Instead, it advises, "Remember your Creator" (Ecclesiastes 12:1). Remembering your Creator is the surefire way to unlock a promising future. While you are young and blessed with happiness, joy, health, and strength, remember the Creator. When all possibilities are open to you, remember that God is your guide.

Let's prepare for the new year of faith. May our memory be renewed, allowing us to eagerly anticipate a new future under God's guidance. Wash away past scars and face future challenges with faith.

In the end, remember, it's not about what the future holds; it's about who holds the future.

# 44

# A CALLING REQUIRES COURAGE

NELSON MANDELA DISPLAYED a remarkable lack of vengeful impulses as he fought against apartheid and racial discrimination. It required tremendous courage for a politician not to seek revenge for the persecution he endured. Mandela spent over twenty years in prison, yet when he became the president of his country, he committed himself to faithfully pursuing his calling rather than seeking retribution.

In 1995, just a year after Mandela assumed the presidency, the Rugby World Cup took place in South Africa. The Black population refused to support the national team as all the players representing South Africa were White. In response, Mandela personally donned a player's uniform and cheered on the team from the stadium. His intention was to dismantle another form of discrimination rooted in a victim mentality within the Black community. Witnessing this act, people of all races rallied behind the national team with a unified voice. Through the courageous actions of a leader devoted to his calling, the nation was able to stand together, setting aside superficial differences.

Those who have positively transformed the world throughout history, like Mandela, share two common traits. First, they discover what is right and just. Second, regardless of the hardships and sacrifices demanded of them, they boldly pursue their calling without giving up. If the former could be categorized as a "calling," the latter can be termed as "courage." Courage pushes us to do what is right at any cost.

A sense of meaninglessness arises when one's life is devoid of a sense of calling. Individuals often spend excessive amounts of time comparing themselves to others and carry the burden of pretense to please those around them. They may take on an overwhelming workload, living their lives bound by time constraints and the pressure to perform.

However, one's calling is as unique as one's fingerprints. There are specific things that individuals are meant to do. A calling does not age. There is no need to conform to the world's standards, nor is there an obligation to unconditionally please others. Instead, there is the freedom to love others as they are, without pretense.

When one lacks the courage to pursue a discovered calling, life loses its meaning. Living in alignment with a calling requires the courage to make alternative choices when necessary. Without courage, individuals are prone to forsake their calling and be swayed by circumstances or other people.

Religious philosopher Paul Tillich once posited that true courage comes from being and accepting oneself. We can rephrase this as "true courage means following the calling that God has given you." By boldly dedicating ourselves to our calling, without being swayed by life's circumstances, we can discover the true purpose of our existence.

When some Pharisees informed Jesus that Herod intended to kill him, Jesus boldly proclaimed, "Go tell that fox, 'I will keep on driving out demons and healing people today and tomorrow, and on the third day I will reach my goal'" (Luke 13:32). Jesus assured us that regardless of any threats from Herod, his plans would never be canceled or diminished. Jesus is not swayed by time and circumstances; he is the master of all things.

Jesus exhibited tremendous courage, unafraid of suffering and death, in order to fulfill the calling God had given him. While people try to avoid an untimely end, for Jesus death represented the culmination of his ministry. Although aware of the wicked plans against him, Jesus chose not to evade death but instead embraced the path of righteousness.

Have you discovered a calling worthy of sacrificing your social status, public acclaim, and even your life? Are you courageously living in pursuit of your calling, unafraid of death? Only those who discover God's personal calling for themselves can live a purposeful life. And when you boldly live according to that calling, your life becomes an instrument used by God to change the course of history.

While we live in pursuit of our calling, it is not hardships but rather temptations that can lead to our ruin. Temptations precede hardships. The same was true for Jesus—he faced three temptations in the wilderness before enduring the suffering of the cross. However, Jesus did not succumb to these temptations. If he had faltered, suffering would not have ensued. The same applies to us. The fact that suffering, which threatens our calling, has not yet arrived signifies that we have already relinquished our calling to temptations. We have forsaken our calling for power, comfort, and honor. We must overcome these temptations that lead us away from our calling. Only then will suffering come our way. And if we courageously hold fast to our calling amid suffering, we will be employed in the great work of God.

# 45

# GOD WILL GUIDE US

❧

PEOPLE USE VARIOUS METHODS when going to a place they have never been before. The first method is to embark on a journey without planning, finding their way through trial and error. The second method is to use a map and compass, enabling them to accurately determine where to go. The third method is to go with someone who knows the way, ensuring that they can find the correct path no matter how complicated or challenging it may be.

The Israelites left Egypt and began an unexpected journey. Not really knowing where they were going, they looked to Moses for guidance, who in turn looked to God. The wilderness was a no man's land, and Israel became a nomadic community. God did not tell Moses to find the Promised Land using a map and compass. Instead, God chose to personally lead his people.

God guided the Israelites traveling through the wilderness with a pillar of cloud during the day and a pillar of fire at night. The cloud shown to Moses was a cloud in the sky, but after the exodus it descended on Mount Sinai and filled it. When the tabernacle was completed, the cloud descended from the mountain and filled the tabernacle and the ground.

God is gradually coming down. Pay attention to the God who comes down from heaven to earth. While God exists in heaven, he is not present there only; he came down to earth to be with his people. The Lord Jesus Christ pitched a tent on this earth through the incarnation as Immanuel, "God with us." Jesus then sent the Holy Spirit, who remains with us as the indwelling presence of God.

For the Israelites, the movement of the cloud represented God's commands. When the cloud moved, the people followed. When it stopped, they also stopped. Their daily routine began and ended with observing the movement of the cloud. They looked to the cloud to know when to start their journey and when to stop and rest. As human beings we look toward the sky, unlike other animals who focus on the ground.

Discerning God's will is not a matter of knowing where to go or what to do, but rather of living in the presence of God moment by moment. When we ask God, "What should I do?" he answers, "Do you not want to come closer to me?" When we ask for a solution to a problem, he says, "Will you not first give me your heart?"

The reason we don't always know where to step in life is that we're not looking to the pillar of cloud in God's presence. Why did God lead the Israelites like nomads following a cloud pillar?

First, God wanted to teach them to trust his guidance, one step at a time, without revealing the entire future. Second, he wanted to teach them to be obedient, whether they understood his command or not. As Erwin McManus said in his book *An Unstoppable Force*, "But the Spirit of God moves like the wind, leaving a still silence where he once blew and beckoning us to where he now stirs. The church must raise her sails and move with the Spirit if we are not to be left behind. It is not enough to simply hang on; we must boldly move forward." Third, God wanted to show them a life of voluntary companionship with the Lord, loving the ever-present God rather than reluctantly following his commands. The ultimate goal of faith is to willingly surrender our will to God.

Living leaves are soft and flexible, while dead and dying leaves are rigid and brittle. Rigidity is a characteristic of death. When we try to live with ourselves in control, our lives become very rigid. Jesus led a thoroughly disciplined life, but it was a gentle and flexible life, not a rigid one filled with stubbornness. May the wandering Christians in the wilderness find joy and delight walking the path of life shown by God.

# 46

# LOVE HAS MANY HUES

ॐ

JUST AS LIGHT PASSING THROUGH A PRISM reveals an array of colors, love also displays a variety of hues. Dwight Moody (1837–1899) expounded on the nine fruits of the Holy Spirit, using love as the foundation. He described joy as love overflowing with delight, peace as love that brings comfort, patience as love endured through trials, kindness as love displayed toward others, goodness as love expressed through action, faithfulness as love persevering through conflict, gentleness as love learned and practiced, and self-control as love honed through discipline.

The reason for interpreting the fruit of the Holy Spirit in this way is found in Galatians 5:22-23, where the word *fruit* is singular: "But the fruit of the Spirit is love, joy, peace, forbearance, kindness, goodness, faithfulness, gentleness and self-control. Against such things there is no law."

Since eight attributes are listed after "love," one would expect to read the plural form "fruits." However, it is deliberately singular, indicating the unity of love. This is not a mistake, because the fruit of the Holy Spirit is the various hues of love.

But the characteristics and colors of love are not limited to just these eight. We can discover even more shades of love in 1 Corinthians 13:4-7: "Love is patient, love is kind. It does not envy, it does not boast, it is not proud. It does not dishonor others, it is not self-seeking, it is not easily angered, it keeps no record of wrongs. Love does not delight in evil but rejoices with the truth. It always protects, always trusts, always hopes, always perseveres."

Why does this description mostly align with but also differ from the fruit of the Holy Spirit mentioned in Galatians? It is because the lives of believers in the Galatian church and the Corinthian church are similar. Regarding the ninefold fruit of the Holy Spirit in Galatians, why does the writer directly emphasize "joy" after "love"? Perhaps it is because the Galatians were living a joyless existence, caught in legalism and devoid of the freedom God intended for them. How could they experience joy without embracing the freedom they had been given?

In contrast, Paul highlights "patience" as the foremost characteristic of love when addressing the Corinthian church. This term, which appears third in Galatians, is given priority in 1 Corinthians. We can observe that for the Corinthian congregation patience—meaning enduring for the long haul—was of utmost importance. Furthermore, in the original text of 1 Corinthians, the word is used as a verb. Although some translations render it as an adjective modifier, the Greek uses the verb form. All the words are written in the present tense, signifying that love is not a past action or a future ideal. Love is meant to be actively demonstrated in the present moment.

The true essence of love is not stagnant; it encompasses diverse colors. It is a genuine action that surpasses mere feelings. In 1 Corinthians, love is depicted as if it were a person. Through this we come to understand that love manifests itself through our actions.

A professor at Johns Hopkins University conducted a study involving two hundred youth, aged twelve to sixteen, who lived in a slum. The purpose was to investigate how they would lead socially healthy lives as adults. Initially, the researchers examined their family environments and abilities, and the findings were disheartening. They estimated that 90 percent of this population would spend most of their lives in jail.

Approximately twenty-five years later, some university students revisited the area to evaluate the accuracy of the research conclusions. Most of the young people investigated had left the town. The students managed to locate 180 of the 200 individuals and were astonished by the results: only four had ended up in prison, while the rest were law-abiding citizens leading regular lives. The initial prediction of the research had been proven wrong.

When interviewed, the individuals were asked how such a result came about. They responded that it was all because of a teacher who had enabled them to thrive. The researchers then sought out the teacher and inquired about his methods. The teacher humbly replied, "I didn't do anything special. I simply loved them." The love of a single teacher changed the lives of hundreds.

In the words of renowned psychiatrist Karl Menninger (1893–1990), "Love is a medicine that cures the diseases of the world." Love possesses a transformative power that can heal the afflictions of the soul. It brings healing not only to those who are loved but also to those who extend love.

In Mitch Albom's book *Tuesdays with Morrie*, a profound conversation takes place between Mitch, who is a student, and Morrie, a professor grappling with the limitations imposed by Lou Gehrig's disease. They delve into the meaning of life, and Morrie imparts a valuable insight: "It's become quite clear to me as I've been sick. If you don't have the support and love and caring and concern that you get from a family, you don't have much at all. Love is so supremely important."

A letter penned by Charles Wesley (1707–1788) to his friend George Whitefield (1714–1770) echoes this sentiment. Wesley expressed the deep anguish that God could use him as an instrument without working inside him. He realized that although God was utilizing him as a vessel, the overflowing love of God was not filling his own heart. Pastors, too, may find themselves in a situation where they are instruments in God's hands but are without God's love in their hearts. While God can bestow gifts on them and employ them as tools, this can also be a source of personal anguish.

When God created the world, it was infused with a myriad of love's vibrant hues. However, sin has disrupted and distorted those colors. Yet, through the love of Jesus Christ, those beautiful shades are being restored. The Holy Spirit, often referred to as the Spirit of Christ, works within us to manifest the resplendent colors of love. We should earnestly desire that the hues of love shine forth, whether it be through our individual lives or collectively as a community.

In this way, love acts as a healing balm for the world, bringing restoration, meaning, and purpose to our lives. It is through love that we can overcome the challenges we face, embodying the transformative power that emanates from the very heart of God.

# 47

# A BUCKET LIST IS A CALLING LIST

֍

HISTORICALLY, THERE HAVE BEEN two common characteristics of people who have brought healthy changes to the world. The first is that they discover their purpose in life, and the second is that they boldly go forward and make sacrifices to accomplish that purpose, no matter how hard and challenging it is. If discovering what one is meant to do is a calling, then boldly moving forward and making sacrifices to fulfill that calling is courage. It takes both calling and courage to change history.

Feeling that life is meaningless is due to living a life detached from one's purpose. Those who do not live according to their purpose exhaust themselves in comparing themselves to others. It is not necessary to be famous to have a purpose. Even if one is not famous or not like others, there is work that one must rightfully do, because purpose is as unique as a fingerprint.

People who do not live according to their purpose carry the burden of hypocrisy and usually try to please others. We have no obligation to make others happy. We have the freedom to love them sincerely just as we are. Those who do not live according to their purpose live a life bound by time and superficial definitions of success. They become obsessed with "accomplishment," compulsively trying to achieve something in the given time or to achieve as much as possible. Purpose does not age. Purpose is unrelated to one's job or even passes when retirement comes.

Feeling that life is meaningless also derives from not having the courage to live boldly according to one's discovered purpose. When lacking courage, people give up their purpose and are led by others or circumstances. To live according to one's purpose, one sometimes needs the courage to make choices and let go of other things. God has given us not a spirit of fear but one of power, love, and self-control (see 2 Timothy 1:7). God gives courage through the Holy Spirit.

Our life's bucket list must become a list of our purposes. Jesus' bucket list had only one item: death on the cross. Jesus demonstrated the unity between purpose and courage, saying, "I must press on today and tomorrow and the next day—for surely no prophet can die outside Jerusalem!" (Luke 13:33). Jesus teaches us that he is not a person swayed by time and circumstance, but rather the master of time and situation. Even though we may plan our day-to-day lives according to our will, we soon realize that life doesn't always go according to our plans and desires. However, Jesus always acted according to his will and plan. Despite threats to his life, Jesus stated that there would be no cancellations or reductions in the work he planned to do. A true bucket list should be based not on mere curiosity but on things we should be joyfully doing, regardless of any hardships we may face.

The apostle Paul's bucket list consisted of spreading the gospel of grace. Even though the Holy Spirit revealed future hardships to him, he did not interpret this as a warning to avoid them. Rather, Paul used the prophecy of suffering as fuel to move forward boldly. With this knowledge, he continued to make the selfless decision to lay down his life for his calling. He used the knowledge not as an excuse to avoid his calling but rather as a source of courage to sacrifice for it.

Only those who discover their God-given calling and who create and execute a bucket list based on that calling can lead a meaningful life. We often crumble under the temptation to deny our calling instead of crumbling under its hardships and threats.

We often give up our calling when faced with the three temptations in the wilderness that tried to bring down Jesus—the temptations of power, comfort, and honor. We forget our calling in the face of these temptations. The fact that no suffering comes to destroy our calling may be because we have already given up our calling because of temptation. We must first overcome the temptations that make us forget our calling. And then, at times, hardships will come. If we don't give up our calling in the face of suffering, but carry it out with bold courage, we can be used by God in great ways. May we, like Jesus and the apostle Paul, walk the path we are meant to walk.

# 48

# WHEN DUTY TRANSFORMS INTO JOY

THERE ARE VERY FEW OF US who look at the duties of our lives and see them as sources of joy. We all deal with duties and responsibilities and there are many that are unavoidable: the duty to care for one's family, the duty to serve one's country, and the duty of an employee's contractual obligations, to name a few. These duties arise because God created humans as social beings.

We can divide people into three categories based on how they approach these duties. The first category includes those who abandon their duties and live recklessly. They live irresponsibly and cause harm to others. The second category includes those who begrudgingly carry out their duties, feeling stifled by the weight of their responsibilities. In the third category are those who transform all given duties into joy and live accordingly. This cannot be achieved by merely adopting a positive attitude toward life. Our hearts don't easily allow us to change duty into joy when faced with suffering. The burden of duty becomes too heavy to bear during adversity. It is difficult to overcome suffering with a sense of duty alone. People who focus only on duty may become despondent when faced with unfair situations or situations they cannot understand.

The gospel of Jesus Christ allows us to approach all duties of life with joy rather than a sense of duty. When Christians, who have experienced the death of their old selves with the death of Jesus Christ on the cross, live in the new life of resurrection, they are granted the ability to change duty into joy. For those who have been restored from death to life, every duty of life becomes a source of joy rather than a burden.

The apostle Paul encouraged slaves of that time who were believers to work diligently and sincerely out of reverence for God, not just to please human masters (see Colossians 3:22-23). It must have been challenging for slaves to treat their masters with the same reverence they would show to God, working wholeheartedly. However, this is the most accurate counsel for believers in the gospel to live with dignity. If slaves who work out of duty do not go beyond this point, they cannot achieve more. But if they change their duties into joy and work wholeheartedly as if serving God, they live a life that exhibits greater dignity than their masters do.

Paul was called to preach the gospel among the Gentiles. Yet there were circumstances that could have forced him to abandon this duty. Nonetheless, he rejoiced. A person who views spreading the gospel merely as a duty would not have been able to find joy in such situations. The ability to remain joyful and free even when one's duties cannot be fulfilled comes from recognizing God's work in every situation. The transformation of duty into joy is achieved not by our own power but by the power of God who works within us, even in the midst of suffering.

The Covid-19 pandemic, as an objective situation, was a major obstacle and hardship in our daily lives. However, through faith, God accomplished good through this pandemic. The pandemic was also a major obstacle to mission work. Yet we must believe that the pandemic can further God's kingdom. This is because God is capable of accomplishing good deeds even in the worst situations.

We must realize that we can be used not only in the form we desire but also in the form we do not want. Before hearing what message the church conveys, people in the world look at how that message is connected to the lives of believers. People want to see the gospel before they hear it. They want to see if those who proclaim the good news are genuinely rejoicing in it. They want to see whether the joy is not only about affirming life but also about carrying even the most difficult burdens with joy.

Such joy is not the emotion of self-satisfaction felt when everything goes according to one's will. It is obtained when we deny ourselves and follow Christ. Despite economic difficulties, unexpected failures and conflicts, and hardships in relationships, we hope to carry any burden with joy while looking forward to God's good work being accomplished through these trials.

# 49

# A FRIEND WHO WILL NEVER LEAVE

꒜

SOUTH KOREA HAS A HIGH SUICIDE RATE, and if at-risk people had just one true friend to share their heart with, they might not give up on life. In a study conducted by sociology professors at Harvard University over nine years, they followed the lives of seven thousand people and found loneliness at the foundation of suicidal ideation. The death rate of the lonely was found to be three times higher than those who had close friendships. People with bad habits who have good relationships live much longer than people with good habits who are lonely. According to a medical report, people with good relationships are four times better at fighting off cold viruses than those who are isolated. People gain strength through healthy relationships.

In Jesus' time, the nickname attached to Jesus was "friend of sinners." Jesus befriended those who collected taxes from their Jewish brethren to give to the Roman Empire through wicked means. At the time, the tax collectors were considered people who had sold their souls, and no proper Jew would want to be their friend. But when Jesus went to the region of Jericho, he met Zacchaeus, the chief tax collector there. People muttered when Jesus said he would stay at his house. Why would Jesus want to stay at a house like that? However, Jesus did not give up on Zacchaeus (see Luke 19:1-10).

When a woman came to Jesus and poured expensive perfume on his feet, wept, and washed them with her hair, it was an unusual event. At that time it was considered very rude for a woman to exhibit such behavior during a meal. It was a strange act that could create scandal. But when people tried to stop her, Jesus said not to. He accepted her offer with pure gratitude, not impure intentions (see John 12:1-8).

People think that being close to such people will diminish their dignity and worth. They want to be friends with people who are worthy. Parents tell their children to make good friends. But Jesus was closer to those who were abandoned and considered worthless, and he invited them to be friends. He associated with people that parents would advise their children not to befriend.

In Matthew 9:10-13, when Jesus was eating with many tax collectors and sinners, the Pharisees questioned his disciples, "Why does your teacher eat with tax collectors and sinners?" Upon hearing this, Jesus replied, "It is not the healthy who need a doctor, but the sick. . . . I have not come to call the righteous, but sinners."

Just as a doctor becomes a friend to the sick to heal their illness, Jesus became a friend to sinners to heal their sins. Not everyone can become a friend to sinners. There are three reasons why Jesus could be the friend of sinners.

First, Jesus hated sin but did not hate sinners. Most people see sin and sinners as one. Even when separating sin from sinners, they hate the sinner and not the sin. However, Jesus saw sin and sinners separately, hating sin but loving the person.

Second, Jesus associated with sinners but did not commit sins with them. When we interact with people who commit sins, we easily fall into sin together. Although learning good deeds is difficult, sins are easily learned. However, Jesus was a friend of sinners but without sin. The religious leaders of the time tried to find fault or sin in Jesus, but all their efforts were in vain.

Third, Jesus interacted with sinners and opened a way for them not to sin anymore. Jesus said difficult words to understand when interacting with sinners: "Your sins are forgiven" (Mark 2:5). This seemed absurd to the people at the time. One can understand forgiving a perpetrator for what that person has done to oneself; when someone sins against me, I have the right to forgive that person. However, if someone sins against someone else, I have no right to forgive. Yet Jesus forgave people as if they had harmed him, saying this to every sinner he met. Declaring forgiveness of sin is something only God can do. Therefore, when someone else does this, it is tantamount to proclaiming oneself to be God.

A true friend can pay a price and make sacrifices on behalf of a friend. The more one sacrifices, the deeper and longer lasting the friendship. Jesus had this to say about a friend's love: "Greater love has no one than this: to lay down one's life for one's friends" (John 15:13).

A true friend gives his life for a friend. Jesus is the one who gave his life to save sinful humanity and became our friend. Couples who truly love each other become friends. Parents who truly love their children become friends to their children. God, who truly loves humanity, becomes our friend. Jesus is that friend.

# 50

# NOT SUCCESS BUT SERVICE!

ONE SPRING MORNING IN THE APRIL OF 2018, I received a phone call from Mrs. Young-ae Kim, who serves as a senior deaconess at our church. She asked me to meet with two senior deaconesses and pray for them. Later that afternoon, I had the privilege of meeting these remarkable women—a dignified eighty-five-year-old with neatly cut white hair and her seventy-two-year-old cousin. Their presence exuded a sense of spiritual dignity, and their life story intertwined with both the joys and sorrows of the Korean immigrant experience.

"We are cousins," one began. "In 1975, we immigrated to the United States with nearly nothing other than a handful of coins for a phone call. An acquaintance picked us up from the airport and took me to a sewing factory. I worked and sustained myself with a small, packed lunch, quenching my hunger with water throughout the day, and relishing a sliver of melon as thin as my eyebrows for an afternoon snack.

"I barely slept, managing with two or three hours of rest a day, as I poured my heart into my work, risking my life to earn enough money to survive. However, the following year I succumbed to exhaustion and found myself hospitalized. In my early forties, I had fallen ill due to malnutrition. Meanwhile, my cousin was attending beauty school and opened a beauty salon. Through sheer determination and tireless effort, we managed to purchase our first home in the United States, built on the fruits of our labor. But one day I began to wonder what God would say to me when I reached heaven. Would he tell me that all I did for him on earth was operate a sewing machine?

"On that very day I made a life-changing decision to dedicate myself to mission work as a Christian missionary. Together with my cousin, I decided to return to our homeland, where we could communicate in our mother tongue. Although an elder from the local church in the United States tried to dissuade us, our pastor assured us that Korea, too, was part of the mission field and encouraged our return. From that point forward, we served as tent-making missionaries for eighteen years at an assisted living facility."

Eventually, with God's guidance, they made the decision to return to the United States. Before embarking on their journey, however, they made a profound choice. They had sold their home in America and purchased an apartment in Seoul many years ago. The proceeds from the sale, combined with their life savings totaled about $900,000. They donated all of it to Handong Global University, saying, "We aim to sow the seeds of our tears and sweat into the university, trusting that God will nurture the students, causing the branches to flourish and bear fruit for countless young individuals. Is there a greater reward than this?"

But they had no place to return to in the United States. So they waited and prayed because they knew that God was telling them to return to America.

After a seven-year wait, their application for an apartment subsidized by the US government was finally approved in 2018. It was a true testament to God's provision and intervention.

"We do not worry about our old age," one said. "We are certain that God will provide everything we need when we return to

America. If God gives us 10 cents, we will use 10 cents. If it is 5 cents, then we will make do with 5 cents. We have grown accustomed to a frugal life. Even if we were to become homeless, God would provide for us."

The US government's monthly assistance amounts to about $1,200, which would enable them to save and pay for the rent for the apartment.

"We have come to realize that if we are content and do not spend unnecessarily, our resources accumulate," one said. "That has been our way of living thus far. I have never owned expensive clothing in my life, always purchasing within the range of $1 to $20 or making do with altered or patched-up old clothes. Despite never dining out or traveling, we have found contentment in our simple life.

"Initially, I had thought about buying some things we needed before returning to the United States, but the Lord spoke to me, saying, 'I have prepared everything you will require.'

"Coincidentally, I was reading the story of Ananias and Sapphira in the book of Acts during that time, which convicted me. My cousin went into her room to pray about the matter at the same time, and God confirmed with her. So we made the decision to surrender it all to God."

As she shared her story, her eyes welled up with tears as she recalled the hardships she had endured in the past. Listening to the heartfelt confessions of these two women, my voice trembled as I prayed for them. My throat grew tight, and my prayers were whispered with difficulty. I simply said, "God, bless these two deaconesses, who have poured out their lives like the woman who broke the alabaster jar. Lord, may their lives bring honor to your name. Protect them throughout their days!"

After hearing their testimony, I asked if I could share their story. I wanted my congregants and the students who received the fruit of their labor and sacrifice to know about their consistent desire to follow God.

Handong Global University, the recipient of their very generous donation, urges its students to "earn money and give to others" and "study hard and give to others" in this era where money has become an idol. I firmly stated that the students of Handong, at least, should hear about their testimony so that they might be encouraged to live their lives according to these sentiments.

The women asked to remain anonymous, so while I am not sharing their names, I felt called to share their testimony. The Lord has prompted me to celebrate the devotion of the women, who lived their lives like the woman who broke the alabaster jar at Jesus' feet.

As I reflect on the extraordinary dedication exemplified by these two women, I am reminded of the life and words of Elizabeth Johanna Shepping, also known as Seo-pyeong Seo. She was a German American missionary who wholeheartedly dedicated herself to serving the Korean people. Shepping poured out her care and love on orphans, unwed mothers, the homeless, and people with leprosy. Tirelessly caring for the Korean people, she established orphanages, clinics, and women's schools. Regrettably, the life of this extraordinary servant was cut short by the ravages of malnutrition. The whole city mourned for the loss of a true servant of God.

The conviction, "Not success but service!" defined her life. Shepping emphasized that the ultimate purpose of our existence lies not in the pursuit of personal success but in wholeheartedly devoting ourselves to sacrificial service.

These women will never be great by the standards of the world. But we know, for certain, that they were good Christians.

# ACKNOWLEDGMENTS

THE ADAGE "A BUSY PASTOR IS A BAD PASTOR" resounds with profound truth. The unrelenting demands of busyness strip away the spiritual depth cultivated through an intimate connection with God. This erosion hinders introspection into one's inner life, leaving the pastor susceptible to trials, temptations, and challenges in navigating the dynamic landscape of contemporary ministry and articulating relevant truths.

In my pursuit to evade the pitfalls of busyness, this book has emerged: a collection of essays crafted in fleeting moments rather than protracted reflections. Many draw inspiration from the writings of venerable spiritual leaders, particularly influenced by the prophetic insights of C. S. Lewis into the postmodern age. The missionary zeal of Lesslie Newbigin, dedicated to communicating Christ's uniqueness amid the postmodern era, serves as a significant wellspring for the content of this book.

The unwavering prayers and support from the elders and members of Onnuri Church have been indispensable in my journey of pastoral growth. My special gratitude extends to Pastor Jong-gil Park and the dedicated pastoral team at Onnuri Church.

I extend deep appreciation to Mrs. Hyung-ki Lee, the late Pastor Yong-jo Ha's wife, for her prayers and encouragement. The indelible influence of the late Elder Young-gil Kim; Mrs Young-ae

Kim, Chairperson for Handong Global Support Program; Chairperson Jung-geun Yoo of the United Nations Academic Impact Korea; and President Do-sung Choi of Handong Global University permeates the essence of this book.

Acknowledgments are due to Rev. In-ho Lee, Rev. Ghap-shin Jung, Rev. Sung-eun Choi, and the collaborative efforts of other pastors at Gospel and City, who are actively engaged in planting and renewing gospel-centered churches in South Korea. My sincere appreciation extends to Dr. Michael Oh, CEO of the Lausanne Movement; Dr. Hyung-keun Choi; and Missionary Cheolho Han. I express profound gratitude to Elder Yong-man Lee for his constant fatherly care, and to Elder Sang-geon Jung for his unwavering dedication to serving CGN. I want to especially commend Pastor Stephen Cha and Pastor Han-kyu Lee for their invaluable role in translating and publishing this book.

My gratitude extends to the editorial team at InterVarsity Press for their decision to publish despite imperfections.

Above all, my profound appreciation goes to my wife, Jung-sun Lee, and our cherished children, Eun-taek and Eun-hye. This book stands as a testament to the abundance and devotion of my wife's love, and I am deeply thankful for the unwavering support and encouragement from my children.

# ABOUT THE AUTHOR

꙰

REVEREND JAE HOON LEE serves as the senior pastor at Onnuri Church, a prominent congregation committed to fulfilling the Great Commission.

*Onnuri*, which translates to "all nations," is dedicated to spreading and embodying the transformative message of the gospel worldwide. Their unwavering commitment to global missions has led to the deployment of 876 missionaries currently serving in seventy-five countries. Moreover, Onnuri Church extends a warm embrace to various ethnic groups coming to Korea, including migrant workers and refugees, by offering worship services and community care service in twenty-one languages across eleven Korean campuses and thirty campuses abroad. Onnuri Church also operates CGN (Christian Global Network), a twenty-four-hour Christian satellite broadcasting network offering programs in seven languages; and A Better World, a non-profit organization dedicated to infrastructure development in thirty-two countries. Onnuri is committed to sharing the gospel with people from all nations.

In addition to his responsibilities at Onnuri Church, Rev. Lee serves as the chairperson of Handong Global University, recognized as the most biblical and transformative university in South Korea. Additionally, Rev. Lee serves the Lausanne Movement as the chair of the Lausanne Korea committee and cochair of the organizing committee for the 2024 Lausanne Congress in Seoul.

Rev. Lee holds academic degrees from Myongji University (BA), Hapdong Theological Graduate School (MDiv), Trinity Evangelical Divinity School (ThM), Gordon-Conwell Theological Seminary (DMin), and Presbyterian University and Theological Seminary (DD).